VITAL CONGREGATIONS— FAITHFUL DISCIPLES

VISION FOR THE CHURCH

Foundation Document

THE COUNCIL OF BISHOPS OF THE UNITED METHODIST CHURCH

Copyright © 1990 by Graded Press.
All rights reserved.

An official resource for The United Methodist Church prepared by the General Board of Discipleship through the Division of Church School Publications and published by Graded Press, 201 Eighth Avenue, South, P. O. Box 801, Nashville, Tennessee 37202. Printed in the United States of America.

Scripture quotations in this publication, unless otherwise indicated, are from the *New Revised Standard Version Bible,* copyright © 1989, Division of Christian Education of the National Council of the Churches of Christ in the United States of America. Used by permission.

For permission to reproduce any material in this publication, call 615-749-6421, or write to Graded Press, Syndication—Permissions Office, 201 Eighth Avenue, South, P. O. Box 801, Nashville, Tennessee 37202. Local churches are granted permission to reprint in church bulletins and newsletters excerpts from the main text of this Foundation Document.

To order copies of this publication, call toll free: 1-800-672-1789. Call Monday–Friday, 7:30-500 Central time or 8:30-4:30 Pacific time. Use your Cokesbury account, American Express, Visa, Discover, or MasterCard.

VISION FOR THE CHURCH

Preface...5
Overview..9
The Gathering of the People of God............................... 15
Praise Be to God... 23
Our Confession as a People of Faith...............................33
Our Freedom in Christ... 45
Hearing the Word of God...51
    Living by the Story of Jesus................................... 54
    Living by the Power of the Holy Spirit....................58
    Living by the Witness of the New Testament Church...............61
    Living by the Stream of Wesleyan Heritage.......................... 66
    Living as Congregations by Memory and Hope.......................74
Claiming Our Baptism..87
Prayers of the Congregation.. 97
Offering Our Response to the Lord................................ 111
    Signs of Vitality in Congregational Life....................113
    Signs of Faithfulness in Discipleship...................... 123
Holy Communion: Sign of Reconciliation and Love.................. 133
The People of God Are Blessed and Sent............................. 141
Appendix A: Glossary.. 149
Appendix B: Consultants...154
Pastoral Letter..158

PREFACE

This *PASTORAL LETTER* and *FOUNDATION DOCUMENT* include both a vision and a call from the Council of Bishops to the people called United Methodist.

We, the bishops, are sharing with the church in these documents a vision of vital congregational life and faithful discipleship, a vision toward which we have been moving during two years of study, prayer, and conferences. We are issuing herewith an urgent call to every local congregation to join us in this process of seeking God's vision for the church and to formulate all that the vision means for the unique local situation where each congregation has been placed for mission and ministry. Our pilgrimage has led us to affirm the hope that every local community of faith will be a vital congregation of faithful disciples whose individual and corporate life are a daily response to the grace of God . . . a response of praise, confession, listening to the word of God, celebrating the sacraments, and going forth day by day to tell the world in speech and actions the good news of God's amazing grace.

The Council of Bishops is sending this message to the church with a sense of great urgency, which is gathered up in the following paragraphs from our *Pastoral Letter:*

> We, the people of God called United Methodist, have come to a critical turning point in our history. The world in which our heritage of faith seemed secure is passing away. We must choose to be faithful to Jesus Christ in our time.
>
> There are many signs within our congregations that we recognize this new era. The realization is dawning on us that we must be more intentional about being the church God calls us to be. The immense suffering of so many people in the world today overwhelms us, but these human hurts also stir our deepest impulse to follow our Master into service and fellowship with those who suffer.
>
> . . . .
>
> We, the bishops of the church, yearn for a vital congregation in every place. We yearn because so many people of our societies, including many in our church, have no vital relationship to God, and are lost: lost to drug addiction, lost to self-centered materialism and self-righteousness, lost to the demonic forces of racism and every form of human oppression—lost to sin. We are concerned that as our

world becomes more secularized, new generations increasingly are bewildered by every form of temptation and desperately need the saving grace of Christ.

These convictions have compelled us to affirm clearly our identity with and support of local congregations as they seek to realize their vision of vitality and faithfulness at this critical time in the church's life and mission. This summons to the church is not a call to implement some new "handed-down" program initiative. It is not intended to be a "quick fix" for the troubles we face. It is an invitation to seek new vision for the church and to discern by disciplined quest ways to make the vision a reality.

A number of helpful resources are available to local congregations in their response to this episcopal initiative. A *Leader's Guide* has been prepared for use by groups involved in study, prayer, reflection, and action. A bibliography of helpful materials is included in the *Leader's Guide*. A glossary of certain words used in the document is included in the *Foundation Document*. An introductory video has been produced to introduce the *Pastoral Letter* and *Foundation Document*. Many program resources related to vital congregational life and faithful discipleship are available from the general boards and agencies of our church.

Many persons have made significant contributions to the preparation of the *Foundation Document*. A two-day consultation in Nashville, Tennessee, and a three-day consultation in Atlanta, Georgia, allowed a panel of bishops to hear thirty consultants, including local church pastors and lay persons, teachers from theological seminaries, staff persons from general agencies, and others with special expertise and experience in the area of congregational life. Each bishop appointed an Area Advisory Committee that involved more than eight hundred laity and clergy across the church in reading and offering suggestions and materials for the *Foundation Document*. Nearly three hundred congregations conducted "A Gathering for Celebration and Discovery" and sent their responses to the Council. The stories, images, and prayers of these congregations are found throughout the book.

The *Foundation Document* is enriched with the hymns, prayers, Scripture, and *Discipline* of the church. All hymns are quoted and numbered in accordance with the new *United Methodist Hymnal*. All Scripture quotations are taken from the *New Revised Standard Version* of the Bible. The 1988 *Book of Discipline* is the source for all disciplinary citations. *Grace Upon Grace: The Mission Statement of The United Methodist Church* is the statement on the mission of the church adopted by the 1988 General Conference.

PREFACE

The Committee on Episcopal Initiatives in charge of this project consisted of Bishops C. P. Minnick, Jr., Chairperson; Judith Craig; Elias G. Galvan; William Boyd Grove; Leroy C. Hodapp; Felton E. May; Emerito P. Nacpil; Richard B. Wilke; and Roy C. Clark, Executive Director.

Dr. Thomas E. Frank, Director of the Rollins Center for Church Ministries at Candler School of Theology, was the research coordinator, consultant, and principal writer of the *Foundation Document*. Helen E. Casey-Rutland served as research associate and designed the material in the outer column of each page. A staff support group assigned by the general secretaries of the General Board of Global Ministries, the General Board of Discipleship, the General Council on Ministries, United Methodist Publishing House, and United Methodist Communications offered essential and invaluable service. We are deeply grateful to all of these persons for the services they rendered to the Council of Bishops in this project and for the resources they prepared and supplied.

—Bishop C. P. Minnick, Jr.
Chairperson
The Committee on Episcopal
   Initiatives for Ministry and Mission
The Council of Bishops

OVERVIEW

We, the people of God called United Methodist, have come to a critical turning point in our history. The world in which our heritage of faith seemed secure is passing away. We must choose now to follow the call of Jesus Christ into a new era. We must seek God's mission for us in a new millenium.

As the turn of the century approaches, we know both the pain and the possibility of these times for our church. The obvious decline in membership of many of our congregations troubles us. We feel burdened by the increasing financial load our congregations are carrying.

But these are only reflections of a wider, rapidly changing picture of Christianity in contemporary culture. We sense that the place of the church in society, particularly in North America and Europe, can no longer be taken for granted. Many of our comfortable assumptions about the support of surrounding culture for Christian beliefs and values have been shaken.

Yet there are also many signs in our congregations that we are recognizing this new era. The realization is dawning among us that we must be more intentional about being the church God calls us to be. The immense suffering of so many people in the world today overwhelms us. But these human hurts also stir us to follow our Master into service and fellowship with those who suffer.

A deep spiritual hunger is awakening our congregations—a longing for communion with our creating, redeeming, and sustaining God. New hymns and prayers for worship are flourishing again after years of drought. Small groups are springing up across the lands, meeting to study the Bible, pray, and wrestle with the tangled questions of our lives. More and more of us are seeking a sense of our own calling to ministry as baptized members of the laity, the people of God. We want our faith and our everyday lives to be vitally connected.

As United Methodism continues to respond to these hungers and challenges, we will become a different church. The Bible provides the most telling images for this movement. We have been accustomed to being at home in the land, to assuming that our societies will be governed by our values and purposes. We have been most comfortable singing the royal psalms, with the king on his throne and people in their proper places.

Now God is calling us to journey. We do not like strange lands; we would rather stay in Egypt than cross the wilderness. But if we risk the journey, our faith will be vastly deepened. We will be trusting in God to give us the manna from heaven and the living water to sustain us. We will find ourselves singing psalms of faith. For we know that those who sing the Lord's song in a strange land will someday gather in the city of God.

Many plans and programs are available to help vitalize our congregations. We celebrate the creativity of local, regional, and national staff in providing plentiful resources for the life and mission of our local churches in all kinds of situations. The fruits of these efforts are promising for the future.

Yet the one above all to whom we must turn is Jesus Christ. For the vitality of our congregations, as of our own lives, is drawn from our life in Christ.

The church is the people called to witness to God's saving action in Jesus Christ. God offers to all who will believe an infinite, redeeming love made known in the cross and in the resurrection of Jesus Christ. As the resurrection promises, God intends to transform this world into a new creation. When that time comes, God will be all in all, and people will live together in wholeness, harmony, justice, and peace. The church is the community of those who expect that new creation, and whose actions point toward its coming. "The kingdom of God has come near," Jesus announced (Mark 1:15), and so the church proclaims today through every word and deed.

"As the Father has sent me, so I send you," declared Jesus (John 20:21). The church's reason for being is to carry forward the ministry of Jesus Christ as a sign of God's mission for the world.

Thus all of us called people of God are evangelists—those who proclaim the gospel. And we are all missionaries—those sent to carry on Christ's ministry of reconciling love. We are sent in the power of the Holy Spirit to make disciples of Jesus Christ. We are sent to call people to repentance, to announce the good news of God's mercy. We are sent to baptize new persons into the fellowship of Christ, and to teach as Christ did the great commandments: love of God and love of neighbor (Matthew 28:19-20).

The central, focal expression of ministry and mission in the name of Christ is found in the local church congregation. The community of believers in each place announces the good news, calls new disciples, nurtures and equips the faithful for their mission, and reaches out in ministry, especially among those who suffer.

Here, in the congregation, the gospel must be made real if we expect it to be made real anywhere. Here, in the congregation, is the time and place to wrestle with basic questions about the nature and purpose of the church. Here, in the congregation, out of the ferment of current issues and the fervency of prayer, will arise a new imagination for the mission of tomorrow's church.

The Spirit is calling us, in all our congregations, to a time of discernment—a time of searching, of self-examination, of listening for God's Word—that we may see the new direction in which God is leading us. We seek a fresh vision for the church that we know can only spring from God's vision for the world. Therefore we ask God for clarity of sight and oneness of will that we may perceive what God would have us do.

We must seek vision for the church in a way that is authentic to our identity as a people of God. Many words and methods are available to us from the surrounding culture to help us plan our work. But often these methods only make us feel distant from God. We need to use our own language and self-understanding as people of biblical faith.

We seek our authentic identity not in order to withdraw from the world, but in order to enter it with greater integrity and clearer sense of purpose. We want to find our distinctive voice. We want to have something to say to the world as a people of God. We want to minister more clearly in the name and spirit of Jesus Christ.

In the pattern of our worship, we have a distinctive way of thinking, praying, and living our way toward God's vision for the church. Worship is the focal point of our fellowship together in congregations. Worship is at the heart of the whole Christian life. We experience a range of attitudes in worship—praise, confession, listening for the Word, praying, offering our response. These same attitudes also shape our daily living. As we move through the routines of everyday life in school, work, home, and community, we find ourselves giving thanks to God for our blessings. We seek God's mercy for our mistakes and limitations. Every day we pray for God's guidance in all things.

Worship helps us form our basic responses to the crises of life as well. We know the power of Jesus Christ to bring comfort in our pain. We seek the presence of Christ to bring hope in our difficulties.

If worship is the pattern for all Christian living, then worship is also the pattern for seeking new vision for the church today. Like worship itself, visions are shared. They express our deepest aspirations. Visions compel us to act with commitment and hope. Worship directs us toward God's vision for the world, revealed in the eloquence of prophets and poets and ultimately in the life, death, and resurrection of Jesus Christ our Lord.

Therefore, a pattern of worship provides the structure for our seeking of "Vision for the Church" in this book. Traditional chapter headings are replaced here with elements of worship. The place of each of these elements and its accompanying attitude in the movement of the book is described on the title page of each section.

We begin by gathering as the people of God—gathering our hearts and minds for the seeking of God's vision for us. Christ calls us together with the announcement that the time has come, the Kingdom is at hand. We must turn around and face the horizon of God's new creation. The turmoil and suffering of the world only makes our calling more urgent. We must prepare ourselves for the new forms of witness that God has in mind for us.

Our first act in seeking vision, as in all things, is to praise God. We give thanks for the abundance of life, for the blessings God showers upon us unasked and undeserved, above all for our redemption in Jesus Christ. We praise God for the witness of faithful disciples in every time and place. We name before God with thanksgiving the ministries of many congregations, which represent the many ways Christians witness to their faith around the world.

We then move into a time of self-examination. We express before God the alienation and fear that lie just beneath the surface of our life together in congregations. We confess our lukewarm faith and our shallow commitment. We ask God to forgive us and reconcile us, to give us the courage to renounce those things that divide us from one another and from the Master in whose name we serve.

God's mercy and pardon follow upon our confession. God is giving us another chance. Despite our failings, we are called to be the church. God still wants to use us as evangelists and missionaries of the gospel.

With our sight cleared of the limitations of our past, we turn toward God's Word as the wellspring of our life and the source of new vision. God's living water is most available to us in the stream of witness that flows from Scripture through our heritage and into the continuing story of our congregations. So we hear again the stories and images of Jesus' ministry. We celebrate the power of the Holy Spirit to build up the church. We discover the nature of the church from its foundations in apostolic times. We remember the distinctive character of the Wesleyan movement. Finally, we tell and hear the stories of our own communities of faith in their witness and service across the years. From these foundational stories we receive springs of life. They give us our identity and refresh us in our calling as servants of the Kingdom.

Our response to the Word of God comes first in the form of baptism. We are beginning to realize the full meaning of baptism as our cleansing and initiation into the people of God. Through our baptism we all receive a vocation. Baptism is the occasion for the Holy Spirit to give us the gifts

OVERVIEW

we need for ministry in Jesus' name. As baptized people we are incorporated into a local church congregation as well. There we take the vows of prayers, presence, gifts, and service that make the ministry to which we are baptized real and concrete.

Our second response to God's Word comes in prayers of petition and intercession. Prayers for the church written by congregations in many places are included at this point in the book as a profound witness to the faith of the people of God called United Methodist.

Our response comes, third, in our offering of signs that Christ is alive in us and Christ's ministry is continued through us. We consider the signs of vitality in congregational life and the signs of faithfulness in discipleship. We look for these signs, not as a checklist by which to be measured, but as marks of the Christian life that we envision and discover by God's grace acting in us.

Fourth, we respond by bringing before God the bread and wine with which God nourishes us for life with Christ. We recognize how deeply we need to commune with Christ through the holy meal in which he promised his presence with us. We see at the table how Christ gathers all of us in all our diversity into one Body. Christ makes us into covenant communities who share his vision of a world made whole. Christ gives us food for the journey, and sends us on our way with strength.

Now the time comes to go into the world with God's blessings. We are sent as ambassadors for Christ—to announce the good news, to make disciples, to go where Jesus went, into the hurts and hopes of the world. God's vision for the world is always before us. Our words and deeds make that vision real in our homes, communities, nations, and world.

Our pattern of worship gives us a model for the distinctive way of being Christian in the world. We can speak of our hope in a language that is our unique gift as Christians to the human community. We are grounded in a clear identity and can enter the troubling issues of the world with integrity and purpose.

Therefore let us join together as people of God in this act of seeking new vision for the church, so that we may discern what God would have us be and do as faithful disciples of Jesus Christ gathered into vital congregations. Through this common act we will be united with one another around the world in proclaiming our hope in Jesus Christ, and affirming our commitment to Christ's ministry and mission today.

THE GATHERING OF THE PEOPLE OF GOD

We gather as Christian congregations on many different occasions, but always in the name of our Lord Jesus Christ. We meet for worship, for study, for fellowship, for action, for prayer.

We gather on this occasion to seek new vision for the church.

Our coming together is precious to us. We assemble from many different walks of life. We have many different interests, needs, and hopes. What a miracle that by God's grace the journeys of our lives intersect at this one place, in the life of our congregation.

How good it is to see one another's face, to know that we are "yet alive" and called together into one family of God. Our gathering affirms that we are a community of caring, of witness to a redeeming Lord, of service to a merciful God.

When we gather we remember that God has drawn us together through the sacred calling of Jesus Christ. We reflect on the world from which we have come, ready to bring our own and others' lives before God in praise and prayer.

As we come together we are expectant, anticipating that God in Christ Jesus will be with us, and that the Holy Spirit will move among us. We come knowing that at any moment, God's Word may touch us and change us and call us to new challenges in the service of the Lord.

So we gather, seeking vision for the church. We seek insights into ourselves, perspectives on our world, and discernment of God's purposes for us and for all creation. We begin in hope and expectation that God will reveal to us what we are called to be and to do in days to come as faithful disciples gathered into vital congregations.

VITAL CONGREGATIONS—FAITHFUL DISCIPLES

In a street in a German town, a brass band plays, announcing that the church is coming together as the people of God for worship.

The old bell at Pleasant Hill Church in Olive Branch, Mississippi, is a permanent part of worship, calling people to church in rain, snow, sleet, or heat, reminding worshipers of the generations of people in years past who also heard this bell and heeded its call.

In the Philippines, where the pastor travels between many congregations in many villages, the footsteps of the pastor arriving in the village are the sign for the United Methodist church to gather for worship.

*The church's one foundation
is Jesus Christ our Lord;
we are his new creation
by water and the Word;
from heaven he came and sought us
that we might ever be
his living servant people,
by his own death set free.*

Now after John was arrested, Jesus came to Galilee, proclaiming the good news of God, and saying, "The time is fulfilled, and the kingdom of God has come near; repent, and believe in the good news." As Jesus passed along the Sea of Galilee, he saw Simon and his brother Andrew casting a net into the sea—for they were fishermen. And Jesus said to them, "Follow me and I will make you fish for people." And immediately they left their nets and followed him. (Mark 1:14-18)

Bells are ringing, instruments are sounding. Footsteps are heard on the paths of the world. In Liberia and Oklahoma, in Manila and New York, in the mountains of Switzerland and the valleys of California, we the people of God called United Methodist are gathering in witness to Jesus Christ our Lord.

Bells are ringing, and the places in which we assemble are as varied as the world's cultures. We meet in huts of woven grass and in stone cathedrals. We gather in groups of twenty and in crowds of two thousand. We lift up our voices in Spanish and in Korean. In every place we praise the Lord.

Instruments are sounding, and the communities in which they are heard are as varied as the world's societies. We are dark skinned and light skinned, prosperous and poor, rooted in the land and displaced from home. We live amid revolution and stability, literacy and destitution. Our instruments call us out to bring our communities and world to God in prayer, so that we might serve them as God would have us do.

Footsteps are beating on sidewalks and paths, on dirt floors and carpeted aisles. The people who gather are as varied as humanity itself. We are male and female, young and old. We are single and married, alone and part of extended families.

Each of us who comes is a unique individual. Each one comes with a unique need. Each comes from the path of a particular journey. Yet the one thing we all have in common is that each has heard, in his or her own way, the call of Jesus Christ. And by the grace of God we are drawn together into a congregation, where Jesus touches our lives according to our needs.

Bells are ringing, and some of us who come cannot remember a time when we did not hear the bells and respond. Some of us who hear the instruments have always walked to the cadence of Christ, as nearly as we knew how. Others of us who hear the bells may always have heard them, but only recently found ourselves in search of the cause of their ringing. Some of us have only now seen how the Holy Spirit can remold and make us in the image of Christ.

Yet others of us are today for the very first time hearing the bells and walking toward God's house. We may not know exactly why we are coming, or for what we are looking. We may not even know the name of the One who calls us here. But some still small voice has set our feet on the road, and we come.

The call of Jesus Christ is as fresh and timely today as it was on the lakeshore two thousand years ago. The time has come, he says to all who would hear him, just as he declared to Martha and Mary, Simon and Andrew, and countless others then. God's rule of healing, reconciliation, and justice, God's deliverance is at hand, right here and now. Repent, let your lives be turned around. Let all your assumptions and ways of doing things be turned upside down. Put your trust in this good news. Follow me, offer yourselves for my leading, and I will show you how to be servants of God's salvation.

Jesus did not tell the disciples where they were going, nor did he explain to them why they were chosen. He simply called them to follow, and they dropped what they were doing and went with him. Will we? Can we still hear this call and respond?

The time has come for our "yes" to Jesus' call.

The time has come for us "modern" people, oppressed by fear and despair, to let God's grace turn us around to face the horizon of God's hope for the world.

The time has come to ask the Holy Spirit to transform the people of God and build us up into a new community of witness. When Jesus proclaimed the time, he was announcing a *kairos*, the fullness of time in which something was about to happen. Indeed his life, death,

THE GATHERING OF THE PEOPLE OF GOD

Called forth from every nation,
yet one o'er all the earth;
our charter of salvation:
one Lord, one faith, one birth.
One holy name professing
and at one table fed,
to one hope always pressing,
by Christ's own Spirit led.

Samuel J. Stone;
adapt. by Laurence Hull Stookey
The United Methodist Hymnal, No. 546

"As a boy, I lived a half mile from the church. There was a corner a quarter mile away that I had to reach before the church bell rang in order to get there on time."

Shabbona Church
Decker, Michigan

If one enters our large sanctuary before the people arrive, there is the distinct feeling that many souls from the past still reside there. The round stained glass window high above the altar; the mahogany baptismal urn; the heavy glass and iron chandeliers; the red seat cushions—much was given in memory of church members or their loved ones. The Library in the corner of the sanctuary holds shelves of books dated clear back to the 1800s. There is a picture of the Trinity Union Sunday School in its heyday. The people look like they are related.

VITAL CONGREGATIONS—FAITHFUL DISCIPLES

We don't know most of these people. They are dead or gone away. Trinity is a new church now. On any Sunday, there are Africans, Afro-Americans, Cambodians, and Anglo-Saxons. On the bulletin board in Fellowship Hall is a photo of each person who registered for our Sunday School last year, black, brown, and white. Above the Sunday School altar is a hand-crocheted picture of Jesus with outstretched hands, a gift from Sr. M. in Liberia. Below the picture reads, "He's Got the Whole World in His Hands."

Trinity Church
Providence, Rhode Island

The sound of constant traffic reminds worshipers in the Church of Manton in Manton, Michigan, of their location on the "main corner" of town, in the center of their world and its needs.

To be shaped by God's grace is to live in covenant as a community of worship and service. Worship is the offering of life to God; it is the central event of church existence. To worship is to draw into focus an entire way of life. Self-giving to God in worship is to praise God with our whole being. Christian service is not a series of isolated actions; to serve is a way of living.

Grace Upon Grace: The Mission Statement
of The United Methodist Church

*When the church of Jesus shuts its outer door,
lest the roar of traffic drown the voice of prayer,
may our prayers, Lord, make us ten times more
   aware
that the world we banish is our Christian care.*

Fred Pratt Green
The United Methodist Hymnal, No. 592

Hope Publishing Co.; 380 S. Main Pl.; Carol Stream, IL 60188.

and resurrection were the first fruits of God's transformation of the world, the completion of which we await in hope.

We live between the times, between the promise and its fulfillment, between the memories of what God has done for us and the hope of God's unfolding will for us. God's new creation is not yet complete, but it is at hand in signs and glimpses. And we await it with expectation in God's own time.

Therefore as in every generation we are compelled to ask: What time is it in the church and the world? What are the signs of God's graceful reign? What kind of sign are we?

Bells are ringing, instruments are sounding. They echo across elegant suburbs and spreading slums, across settled towns and refugee camps, across crowded cities and open countryside. They are not always easy to hear.

The world at the end of the twentieth century is both deeply restless and profoundly paralyzed. Everywhere we hear the cries of pain and suffering. Everywhere we hear the cries for economic justice, for political participation, for relief from violence and war, and above all, for hope in a meaningful life.

The traditional social order is everywhere under challenge. Ethnic groups across Asia chafe under domination and call for autonomy. The poor of Latin America call for land reform and labor that holds some promise of escape from the treadmill of poverty. Europeans call for a new politics of self-determination in free societies. North Americans call for relief from the onslaught of drugs and for assistance to a growing number of homeless people. Africans call for education, political stability, and a fair opportunity to trade in the world's economy.

But the world's institutions seem strangely immobilized. Grain rots on one side of the globe while people starve on the other. The environment of air, water and land continues to deteriorate while parliaments debate the economic effects of pollution control. Emergency aid is tangled in bureaucracy and political conflict.

What time is it in the world? Much of the answer depends on where one is standing on this globe, and the point of view of one's own culture. Yet clearly the world is in a time of upheaval. A revolution or turning upside down is underway or on the horizon in every society. Technology, economic change, and political unrest are reshaping the world's traditions.

This is a pregnant time, a time of waiting, so full it seems everything is at risk. The apostle Paul wrote of such a time. "We know that the whole creation has been groaning in labor pains until now," he told the Christians in Rome (Romans 8:22). "We wait for it with patience" (verse 25).

The world both fears and hopes for what is to be born, and we as people of God are diverse in our own outlooks. Some people despair of human life holding any ultimate promise. Some teach that this world will be destroyed and only true believers will be saved for a paradise somewhere else. Some argue that human beings are responsible for their own destiny, and that they certainly have the intelligence and technology to create a better world.

Some of us hold fast to our faith that God created the world and intends to guide it to fulfillment. Some suggest that the revolutions currently upsetting the social order are far closer to God's rule of justice than anything in the past. Some believe that God is working through the advancement of human knowledge to complete the creation as God intended it.

Disagreement on how to read the signs of the times is nothing new. Jesus warned his followers not to fall into speculation on the one hand nor to fall asleep on the other. "You know neither the day nor the hour," he declared (Matthew 25:13), and it is not for us to know. What is for us, in the meantime, is to follow where Jesus leads us as a community of witness and service.

God is raising up a people with a new name, a people of God, the church of Jesus Christ our Lord. God is calling the church into ministry for this time, to give its witness as only the church can do.

For the church is born of water and the Spirit (John 3:5), purified and raised to life in Christ, gifted and empowered to serve in Christ's name. By water and the Spirit the church is bold to announce the good news, to

THE GATHERING OF THE PEOPLE OF GOD

The village of Massinga in central Mozambique is normally a sleepy country town of about one thousand people, with rural activity, a few small shops, a market, an administrative center, a school, and a couple of small churches.

Now the village has swollen to over ten thousand people who live in makeshift huts spread around to a distance of fifteen kilometers outside the village. These displaced persons have lost all the few possessions they ever had. Their homes and villages have been burned. They come from as far away as two hundred kilometers to "live" in this reasonably secure place.

In the middle of this confusion of destitute people are the pastors and the Superintendent of the District of Massinga of The United Methodist Church. A good shade tree is chosen for the place of worship. Members follow the pastor's guidance in worship. Others who had not been members, find reassurance in worshipping. They sing, "He arose, He lives, Halleluia, Christ arose."

The way of Christ gives hope to a destitute people who have no other salvation. The pastors and faithful members share their faith with the suffering and hopeless, for in Christ there is a future that will be better and brighter.

Now on the day called Sunday there is a meeting of all those who live in cities or in the country, and the memoirs of the apostles or the writings of the prophets are read as long as time allows. Then, when the reading has stopped, the person presiding gives verbal instructions and challenges the imitation of good things. Then we all stand up together and send up prayers.

Then, as I said before, when we have stopped praying, bread and wine mixed with water are brought, and the person presiding sends up prayers and thanksgivings, insofar as he is able, and the

VITAL CONGREGATIONS—FAITHFUL DISCIPLES

people assent, saying, "Amen!" Then there is a distribution and reception of the elements to each, and what is left is taken by deacons to those not present.

Persons who are well to do and wish to do so each give whatever they choose, and the collection is distributed by the person presiding. He takes care of orphans and widows and those in need on account of sickness or for some other reason and those who are in prisons and aliens who are passing through and, in a word, all those who are in need.

But we all meet together on Sunday, since it is the first day, on which God made the world, transforming darkness and matter, and since Jesus Christ, our Savior, was raised from the dead on that day.

Justin Martyr
Apology (around A.D. 153)

O Spirit of the living God,
thou light and fire divine,
descend upon thy church once more,
and make it truly thine.
Fill it with love and joy and power,
with righteousness and peace;
till Christ shall dwell in human hearts,
and sin and sorrow cease.

Henry H. Tweedy
The United Methodist Hymnal, No. 539

Holbrook Church in Holbrook, Arizona, was established in 1902, meeting first in the historic Bucket-of-Blood Saloon before building the current fellowship hall in 1912.

invite people to receive new life in Jesus Christ and set out on the adventure of discipleship, to risk the tasks of justice and reconciliation.

Across the church we know a hunger for vitality, for the freshness of baptism into Christ's company of disciples and for the purifying and inspiring fire of the Holy Spirit. We long to find our distinctive voice as witnesses of God's will for this earth. We yearn for the grace to be salt, light, and yeast, catalysts of hope in a hurting world (Matthew 5:13-16).

Our hunger for vitality makes us restless with our own immobility as a United Methodist church. We share a malaise that we all know uniquely in each place, a deep uncertainty about our role in society. United Methodism and its predecessor denominations (The Evangelical United Brethren and The Methodist Church) have not grown significantly in membership beyond "biological" growth since well before 1900. That is, our new members have been predominantly our own children.

Meanwhile the North American and European culture that supported belonging to a church, as an expression of good citizenship if nothing else, has changed dramatically since World War II. Most contemporary North Americans claim that they have reached their religious beliefs independent of any congregation. The post-war generations have proven much less likely to be active in a church unless it meets the needs of their religious journey.

Moreover, we can hardly keep up with the social crises that confront us. In every region there are giants in the land before whom we feel like grasshoppers (Numbers 13:33): famine, militarism, unemployment, poverty, racial injustice, broken families, drugs, consumerism. We feel ourselves burdened by multiplying cries for help, for moral guidance, for service.

Truly we stand at a critical turning point in Christian history. The only place to turn is to Jesus Christ, and to a radically new understanding of what Jesus asks of us. The malaise of a shrinking denomination is no match for the despair of this hurting world. And our times are pushing us to find a whole new way of being the church.

The time has come for us to say, "Here am I; send

THE GATHERING OF THE PEOPLE OF GOD

me!" (Isaiah 6:8). The time has come for us who comprise the United Methodist branch of the church, with roots in a lively movement of conversion and holy living, to ask of God a new imagination for responding to Christ's call today.

By the grace of God, we receive our calling and task not simply as individuals but as congregations of the faithful. We are assembled at God's beckoning to be united in love and strengthened to serve.

We come together to watch and pray, to read the signs of our times, to attend to God's Word, to be nourished by the bread of life, and to discern our call as witnesses of God's kingdom. The call still comes, as fresh and timely as on the first day that Jesus ever proclaimed his news. And because it is Jesus' call, there is promise of life in him that surpasses anything we can ask or imagine.

A new imagination for tomorrow's church will arise by God's grace from the creativity and vitality of congregations who find their life in Christ. The local church truly is the church through whose ministries the reign of God must be made known if we expect that reign to be known anywhere. Worshiping, witnessing, serving communities of faithful disciples are Christ's living body in the world. United in one Spirit, bound together in a connectional covenant of mission, they are instruments of God's world-encompassing work.

We live between the times, between the promise of God's new creation and its fulfillment. Congregations exist because Jesus has not come back yet to fulfill that promise. Congregations live in the mean-time, caught between the despair and hope of contemporary life. But this is the gift the Spirit gives us: to have a word from the Lord to speak, to have the courage to act, to enjoy the easy yoke and light burden of joyously and unreservedly carrying on Christ's ministry of reconciling love (Matthew 11:28-30).

And as John Wesley so fervently believed, "the best of all is, God is with us." We do not have to rely on ourselves to get free from our malaise. Jesus Christ frees us if we trust him. Indeed, our very immobility in the

---

Come, we that love the Lord,
and let our joys be known;
join in a song with sweet accord,
join in a song with sweet accord
and thus surround the throne,
and thus surround the throne.

We're marching to Zion,
beautiful, beautiful Zion;
we're marching upward to Zion,
the beautiful city of God.

Isaac Watts, Robert Lowry
The United Methodist Hymnal, No. 733

Our recognition of who we are (and whose we are) leads us to a strong sense of responsibility for the care of others. We are followers of Christ. Our unity in the face of adversity leads us to minister not only to those within our congregation, but also among those in our immediate and world communities.

Garber Church
New Bern, North Carolina

One young redheaded boy came in a few minutes late during the announcements that preceded worship. Catching the pastor's eye and smile, he ran down the aisle and jumped into the pastor's arms for a big hug.

Resurrection Church
Durham, North Carolina

Missional vision is not created by the church, rather it is given to the church by God's saving activity in and on behalf of the world.

Grace Upon Grace: The Mission Statement
of The United Methodist Church

VITAL CONGREGATIONS—FAITHFUL DISCIPLES

*Be thou my vision, O Lord of my heart;
naught be all else to me, save that thou art.
Thou my best thought, by day or by night,
waking or sleeping, thy presence my light.*

Ancient Irish;
trans. by Mary E. Byrne;
versed by Eleanor H. Hull
The United Methodist Hymnal, No. 451

*Sois la semilla que ha de crecer,
sois estrella que ha de brillar.
Sois levadura, sois grano de sal,
antorcha que debe alumbrar.*

*You are the seed that will grow a new sprout;
you're a star that will shine in the night;
you are the yeast and a small grain of salt,
a beacon to glow in the dark.*

Cesareo Gabaraín
The United Methodist Hymnal, No. 583

© 1979, Cesareo Gabaraín. Published by OCP Publications, 5536 NE Hassalo, Portland, OR 97213. All rights reserved. Used with permission.

You are the salt of the earth; but if salt has lost its taste, how can its saltiness be restored? It is no longer good for anything, but is thrown out and trampled under foot.

You are the light of the world. A city built on a hill cannot be hid. No one after lighting a lamp puts it under the bushel basket, but on the lampstand, and it gives light to all in the house. In the same way, let your light shine before others, so that they may see your good works and give glory to your Father in heaven.

Matthew 5:13-16

face of the world's anguish may be the opening God needs to reach us with new vision.

The call of Jesus Christ sets us free to turn around:

—from paralysis to **movement,** enlivening our mission in his name. Methodism began as an evangelical renewal movement among the laity, centered on the personal reality of God, holiness of living, and active love for the poor and distressed. The dynamism of that movement is as available to today's church as it was in the eighteenth century.

—from amnesia to **remembering,** as the story of God's people liberated from bondage and empowered to serve comes alive for us. We see our own story reflected in Scripture. We are a people enslaved, helplessly bound by forces beyond our control. We are a wilderness people looking for water and for bread to sustain us. We are a lukewarm church, tired of the risks to which Jesus leads us. But as the Lord has redeemed the faithful people of every age, so the Lord will redeem us. This is our story too.

—from numbness to **creativity,** as we become a sign to the world that God is alive and God's promise is real. The Holy Spirit is blowing among us to stir a new imagination for the church. We are blessed with countless gifts and resources. All we lack, and by God's grace will receive, is the creativity to match those gifts with the world's needs.

—from nostalgia to **vision,** looking toward God's transformation of all creation. While the past is rich with our heritage, we cannot live in its sphere. Ours is to seek new vision—God's vision—for the church God calls us to be tomorrow.

Bells are ringing, instruments are sounding. The footsteps of God's people echo across the world. The time has come for the church—faithful disciples assembled in vital congregations—to be the salt, light, and yeast of the Kingdom. Christ is calling us into new life. And when we follow, we will find Jesus already there ahead of us, offering signs of that new creation that in God's own time will come.

PRAISE BE TO GOD

Above all else, before all else, we praise the Lord.
We praise God, the source of life who sustains us in every season. We praise Jesus Christ in whom we have life abundantly. We praise the Holy Spirit through whom we are given wind and flame that make our lives new.
An attitude of praise is our distinctive mark as Christians. Our hymns and prayers witness to what God has done for us. Our praise points to the love of God so clearly that those who have not heard the promise of salvation will seek to know God's grace for themselves.
In everything we give God the glory. Not that we are untroubled or naive about the needs and crises of the world. But we know that nothing can separate us from the love of God made known in Jesus Christ. We trust that in God's providence the world is redeemed and a new creation is at hand.
Therefore we praise the Lord and bless God's holy name every time we gather, in every circumstance of life. Especially we thank God for the assemblies of the faithful in every land who sustain us in the Christian life and together make a global witness to God's salvation.
Above all else, before all else, we praise the Lord. For in God alone, and in God's transcendent purposes for the world, may we find the vision for the church that we so earnestly seek.

VITAL CONGREGATIONS—FAITHFUL DISCIPLES

God, whose love is reigning o'er us,
source of all, the ending true;
hear the universal chorus
raised in joyful praise to you.
Alleluia, Alleluia,
worship ancient, worship new.

William Boyd Grove
The United Methodist Hymnal, No. 100

All thy works with joy surround thee,
earth and heaven reflect thy rays,
stars and angels sing around thee,
center of unbroken praise.
Field and forest, vale and mountain,
flowery meadow, flashing sea,
chanting bird and flowing fountain,
call us to rejoice in thee.

Henry Van Dyke
The United Methodist Hymnal, No. 89

As you enter the sanctuary there is a large rubber doormat that reads in large block letters "DON'T GIVE UP." A myth grew up around this mat that many years ago a man was walking to the river, two blocks from our church, to throw himself off the bridge. He came in for a moment of prayer, saw that mat, and knew it was addressed to him. He talked with the minister, joined the church, found a job, and returned to his family. Two years ago, when our

Amen! Blessing and glory and wisdom
and thanksgiving and honor
and power and might
be to our God forever and ever! Amen.
(Revelation 7:12)

Holy, holy, holy Lord, God of power and might, heaven and earth are full of your glory.
Hosanna in the highest.
(from A Service of Word and Table I,
The United Methodist Hymnal, page 9)

From every land, in every language, voices join in a symphony of praise to God. Because God is, we are. Because God is life, we have life. Because God is love, we have life abundantly.

We worship God who brought forth creation out of nothing, who choreographed the joyful dance of all the creatures, who breathed life into humankind. "[God], / who formed the earth and made it, / (he established it; / he did not create it a chaos, / he formed it to be inhabited!)" (Isaiah 45:18).

Our God sustains the universe for purposes that are a holy mystery to us, but to which we give names such as love and joy. Nothing can explain our existence but that we and all creation are an overflowing of the abundance of God's grace. Nowhere is that abundance more apparent than in the life-giving words and acts of Jesus Christ whom we worship as God's Son.

God continues to create, to unfold new possibilities for us and for our world. For God has promised the transformation of all into a new creation in which death gives way to life and suffering to redemption. We await that transformation with hope.

We testify to God who delivers people from oppression, who breaks loose the bonds of slavery, who sets us free for faithful stewardship of the lands God has given us. As once God parted the waters to lead Israel out of bondage and stayed by them in cloud and fire, so now God comes "to proclaim liberty to the captives, / and release to the prisoners" (Isaiah 61:1; Luke 4:18).

We testify to God who stands by us in the wilderness

and provides sustenance for the journey. As once God showered manna from the heavens to feed the hungry people, and brought forth a spring of water from the rocks of Meribah to quench their thirst (Exodus 16; 17), so now in the breaking of bread and the sharing of "a cup of cold water" (Matthew 10:42), God is with us.

We testify to God who in the life, death, and resurrection of Jesus Christ has offered healing and hope for all who put their trust in the name of the Lord. For Jesus Christ is the first fruits of a new creation in which death is conquered and life in God flourishes eternally.

By the power of the Holy Spirit we are called and given gifts to live in the way of Christ as his disciples. Therefore we sing, "Spirit of Holiness, let all thy saints adore thy sacred energy, and bless thine heart-renewing power" (*The United Methodist Hymnal*, No. 88).

We are creatures of a living God, the one God, "I AM WHO I AM" (Exodus 3:14). We are called into covenant with the God of Abraham, Isaac, and Jacob, the God of Sarah, Miriam, and Ruth, the God made known to us in Jesus Christ. This is God whose praise we sing, in whom we live and move and have our being. This is God for whose glory we live.

Christian congregations are above all else gatherings of praise and thanksgiving. They exist because God is, to give witness that God is. They exist to praise God, to give witness to all that God has done. They exist to give God thanks, to give witness to all the blessings showered upon us in abundance. We who gather in congregations worship God because we simply have to: Our worship is the overflow of our joy in God's gifts of life and salvation.

Christian congregations exist because God calls them into being. They exist because God loves the world, and wants that love to be shown. They exist because God needs bearers of the light, messengers of God's mercy and justice. We who gather in congregations serve God because we simply have to: Our service is an outpouring of God's continuing mission to save and transform the world.

As long as there are congregations of faithful praise

janitor of 40 years retired, he told the congregation that he was that man.

Snyder Memorial Church
Jacksonville, Florida

The God of Abraham praise, who reigns enthroned above,
Ancient of Everlasting Days, and God of love;
Jehovah, great I AM! by earth and heaven confessed,
I bow and bless the sacred name forever blest.

The Yigdal of Daniel ben Judah
para. by Thomas Olivers
The United Methodist Hymnal, No. 116

Five years ago, some members of a "Hauskreis" (group gathering regularly in the house of one of its members) took it upon ourselves to build a congregation. None of us had any experience in starting a new congregation. Sometimes we lacked courage, ideas, and even money. Ministers and others from nearby helped us get started.

But we got so much help from our Lord Jesus Christ as never before! That now a congregation exists, little but alive, is surely not only due to various initiatives on our part but is a gift of our Lord.

Überlingen/Lake of Konstanz Church
Konstanz, West Germany

But you are a chosen race, a royal priesthood, a holy nation, God's own people, in order that you may proclaim the mighty acts of him who called you out of darkness into his marvelous light.

VITAL CONGREGATIONS—FAITHFUL DISCIPLES

*Once you were not a people,
   but now you are God's people;
once you had not received mercy,
   but now you have received mercy.*

1 Peter 2:9-10

*God of many names, gathered into One,
in your glory come and meet us, moving endlessly
   becoming;
God of hovering wings, womb and birth of time,
joyfully we sing your praises, breath of life in every
   people,
Hush, hush, hallelujah, hallelujah!
Shout, shout, hallelujah, hallelujah!
Sing, sing, hallelujah, hallelujah!
Sing God is love, God is love!*

Brian Wren
The United Methodist Hymnal, No. 105

Hope Publishing Co.; 380 S. Main Pl.; Carol Stream, IL 60188.

*When Christ shall come with shout of acclamation
and take me home, what joy shall fill my heart.
Then I shall bow in humble adoration,
and there proclaim, my God, how great thou art!*

*Then sings my soul, my Savior God to thee;
how great thou art, how great thou art!
Then sings my soul, my Savior God to thee;
how great thou art, how great thou art!*

Stuart K. Hine
The United Methodist Hymnal, No. 77

© Copyright 1953 S.K. Hine. Assigned to Manna Music, Inc. Renewed 1981 by Manna Music, Inc. 25510 Avenue Stanford, Suite 101, Valencia, CA 91355. International copyright secured. All rights reserved. Used by permission.

*Amazing grace! How sweet the sound
that saved a wretch like me!
I once was lost, but now am found;
was blind, but now I see.*

John Newton
The United Methodist Hymnal, No. 378

everywhere or anywhere, there will be signs that God is, and that God will redeem the world as God has promised to do. Christian congregations are found in every part of the globe, worshiping in many different forms, singing in various tunes, reading the Bible in varied languages. The wonder is that in all their diversity, Christian congregations worship the one God whose Spirit has the power to unite them. Their many voices make one chorus of praise and thanksgiving.

Indeed every congregation giving praise to God is joining in a story that began long before it existed and will continue long after it is gone. For in praise we are joined by a great cloud of witnesses in the faith, the communion of all the saints, the faithful worshipers of God in every age and every place (Hebrews 12:1).

And in the fullness of time all those voices will be joined together in eternal praise at the throne of God. Then we shall see God face to face, and there will be no more night and day, for God alone will be our light and God alone our glory (Revelation 22:4-5).

We give thanks to God for the witness to this promise given us in our Christian heritage. In every generation there have been those who gather in the name of Jesus Christ. From them we have received a rich tradition of prayer and song, of sacrament and creed.

As United Methodist Christians, we give thanks for the heritage of John and Charles Wesley. We joyfully claim our inheritance from them, especially their assurance of God's grace. As the Wesleys found in their own lives, God's grace is prevenient, going before us, preparing us and leading us to faith in Christ. By God's grace we are justified, assured of salvation in Christ if only we throw ourselves on God's mercy. In God's grace we are sanctified and prepared for Christian living. And through the power of God's sustaining grace we are made holy, going on to perfection in love. We are assured of God's grace at every step of our journey.

We name before God with gratitude those witnesses to this grace-filled faith whose energy and imagination gave the Wesleyan movement its dynamism. Some are known to us: Susanna Wesley and Thomas Coke, Francis Asbury and Harry Hosier, Barbara Heck and

Richard Allen, Philip William Otterbein and Jacob Albright. Many others are not known to us, their names forgotten, yet their witness lives on in the mission of the church.

We celebrate the gifts and strengths of world Methodism as a movement that embraces the globe. We thrill to our songs of salvation, and take joy in the many languages that "spread through all the earth abroad the honors of [God's] name" (*The United Methodist Hymnal*, No. 57). We are thankful for the determination and practical bent that has allowed the Christian faith in its Methodist form to adapt and thrive in many cultures and circumstances.

We praise God that congregations of United Methodists worship and serve often against all odds, at great risk, giving God thanks in spite of immense suffering. Many congregations live close to the edge of persecution, of famine, peril, and sword (Romans 8:35). Yet they endure, serve, and make a difference in people's lives. They are truly the body of Christ broken for the salvation of the world.

We are thankful to God for the countless ways in which congregations of United Methodists serve the Lord. Nearly four million people in nations all around the globe assemble in over 42,000 United Methodist local church congregations every Sunday. Each gathering is uniquely the church of Jesus Christ in that place. And each has its own calling to be fulfilled, its own ministry and mission in the name of Jesus Christ.

May we be sustained by your strength and warmed with your love as we face our life together in community.

May we walk in the beauty of the world you have entrusted to us and may we see with open eyes and hearts the stars and snowflakes and chickadees and sparrows.

May we be listeners and doers, worthy instruments and partners in your new creation.

In the same faith and belief of our brothers and sisters here and abroad and through centuries of recorded and unrecorded time, we pray. Amen.

College Avenue Church
Manhattan, Kansas

May the God of steadfastness and encouragement grant you to live in harmony with one another, in accordance with Christ Jesus, so that together you may with one voice glorify the God and Father of our Lord Jesus Christ.

Romans 15:5-6

**THEREFORE WITH JOYFUL HEARTS
LET US GIVE THANKS FOR THESE
UNITED METHODIST CONGREGATIONS . . .**

Central Trinity Church in Zanesville, Ohio, the main distributor of USDA surplus food in Muskingum County, where over 1100 families receive food regularly through the efforts of the congregation.

Our Saviour's Church in Schaumburg, Illinois, where worshipers form a circle around the altar to receive Communion.

The churches in Konstanz and Radolfzell, West Germany, where prayer is the main priority for these small, young congregations.

Folsom Memorial Church in Worthington, Indiana, where the congregation raised money to defray the medical bills of two critically ill persons in their community.

Page Memorial Church in Biscoe, North Carolina, where a new Sunday School class for mentally handicapped adults has recently been started.

The church in Linton, North Dakota, where, in the midst of two years of drought, members support one another in the challenge of staying financially afloat.

Wesley Church in Olongapo, The Phillipines, where the congregation operates an elementary school and participates fully in mission evangelism in the district.

First Church on Interstate 30 in Prescott, Arkansas, where stranded motorists and travelers can find shelter, food, clothing, and financial help.

St. Mark's Church in Iowa City, Iowa, where a Parish Nurse program provides coordinated health care and attention to ill persons in the community.

Wesley Church in Trenton, Missouri, where, in the midst of declining population and employment due to the farm crisis, ice cream socials raise money for families in need.

Alamo Heights Church in San Antonio, Texas, where one hundred of the church leaders made a special commitment to prayer for the life and mission of the congregation.

Wintersville Church in Wintersville, Ohio, where the

Arm of Concern ministry offers financial assistance to those hit hardest by the closing of the steel mills.

Wesley Chapel Church in New Albany, Indiana, where Sunday evening altar hour offers an opportunity for prayer at the altar.

First Church in Bluefield, Virginia, where special fifth Sunday mission offerings support the Salvation Army, the Rescue Squad, a local rescue mission, a community high school's "Project Graduation," and other outreach programs.

Randolph Memorial Church in Kansas City, Missouri, where name tags enhance the sense of caring in the congregation.

S. Trowen Nagbe Church in Sinkor, Monrovia, Liberia, where the congregation provides ministries of prayer, music, and service to high school and college students who migrate to Monrovia in search of education.

Osceola Church in Osceola, Iowa, where members give time and energy to the Heifer Project.

Northbrook Church in Roswell, Georgia, where banners that the children made add color to the walls of the sanctuary and serve as a reminder of the gifts children bring.

First Church in Flemingsburg, Kentucky, where a puppet ministry enriches the life of the congregation.

Trinity Church in Ruston, Louisiana, where members are preparing to build a second Habitat for Humanity home.

Brush Church in Brush, Colorado, where an annual spring festival enhances fellowship and sharing among members.

Bagby Memorial Church in Grayson, Kentucky, where a prayer chain continues through the week the prayers offered during Sunday worship.

The United Methodist Women of Nigeria, whose meetings are filled with dancing, singing, study, reports, and worship culminating in a joyous collection of the offering that takes four hours.

Central Church in Atlanta, Georgia, where an enrichment program for local youth includes computer literacy, Afro-American history, and trips to museums and other points of interest.

VITAL CONGREGATIONS—FAITHFUL DISCIPLES

First Church in Oakdale, Louisiana, where a monthly offering buys personal items and medicine for local nursing home residents.

The Church of the Cross in Port Byron, Illinois, where an eternal flame reminds those in the sanctuary that God is always present.

The Church of the Servant in Oklahoma City, Oklahoma, where the sanctuary is alive with plants, rocks, trees, and banners, providing an atmosphere of beauty and openness in which to worship.

Aldersgate Church in Montgomery, Alabama, which annually sends a group to Costa Rica to work and learn in mission.

The Church in Nyabugoga-Gitega, Burundi, where in seven years, the membership has grown from four to four hundred, with an average attendance of five hundred fifty.

First Korean Church in Chicago, Illinois, where people gather at a 6:00 A.M. service each morning for prayer.

Moultonboro Church in Moultonboro, New Hampshire, where a prayer circle helps pull people through times of grief and separation.

First Church in Pensacola, Florida, where two Sunday worship services—one informal, one formal—embrace the broad range of worship needs in the community.

Hockessin Church in Hockessin, Delaware, where each year youth and adult work teams go to serve in Appalachia through the Appalachian Service Project.

First Church in Baguio City, The Philippines, where outreach in the city includes a regular prison ministry, a large choir, a weekly religious radio program, and strong campus and tourist ministries.

Hope Church in San Diego, California, where a ministry of prayer and healing is central to the congregation's identity.

Drew Church in Carmel, New York, where a Thrift Shop helps persons buy low-cost, quality clothing.

Weymouth Church in East Weymouth, Massachusetts, which provided Christmas food, clothing, toys, and "something extravagant, like perfume" to fourteen homeless families.

Ensley Church in Pensacola, Florida, where church members made daily visits to a young mother who broke her neck and needed care for her children during her recovery.

Trinity Church in Lakewood, California, where a drug addict and his family found love and support as they struggled to regain health and stability.

Downey Church in Downey, California, where a church-sponsored nursery school offers high quality child-care for both church members and the community.

Shepherd of the Valley Church in Hope, Rhode Island, where a special offering was taken for a family left without parents.

The church of St. Thomas, Pennsylvania, where two offerings are taken each Sunday: one for the regular budget and benevolences; a second to give away to meet local, national, and international needs through the Second Mile Mission Fund.

Aldersgate Church in Tulsa, Oklahoma, where large banners in the sanctuary celebrate the different liturgical seasons of the church year.

Janes Church in Brooklyn, New York, where the congregation rallied to rebuild after their building was destroyed by fire.

The church in Massinga, Mozambique, where the pastors distribute donations of food and clothing to the many destitute refugees living in the area.

First Church in Portsmouth, New Hampshire, which is working to make its facilities accessible to all persons.

Gethsemane Church in Houston, Texas, where English As a Second Language Classes make a positive difference in this ethnically changing neighborhood.

First Church in Rector, Arkansas, where those who can no longer attend church participate over the phone each Sunday in the Conference Call Sunday School Class.

Trinity Church in Lafayette, Indiana, where a Tenebrae service brought participants closer to God.

OmakRiverside Church in Omak, Washington, where the congregation joins with other congregations in the Greater Okanogan Group Ministry.

VITAL CONGREGATIONS—FAITHFUL DISCIPLES

- St. James Church in Little Rock, Arkansas, where members have supported a person in the congregation who has tested positive for the AIDS virus.
- Ginghamsburg Church in Tipp City, Ohio, where the Administrative Council works by consensus as all seek the mind of Christ for their life together in the body.
- The churches of Poland, Czechoslovakia, Hungary, Yugoslavia, and Bulgaria, where political changes have brought not only social upheaval, but also new opportunities for witness and worship.
- Cross Roads Church in Phoenix, Arizona, which sends work teams to the US/Mexican border.
- Simpson Church in Minneapolis, Minnesota, a member of the Southside UM Coalition (four inner-city UM churches), where members work together to address the urgent needs of the inner city.
- Second Grace Church in Detroit, Michigan, a congregation created by the merger of two congregations—one Black, one White—where special Lenten services and meals nourish their life together.

Thanks be to God for these and a multitude of other ministries we United Methodists have been given by the grace of God.

OUR CONFESSION AS A PEOPLE OF FAITH

We have gathered in the name of Jesus Christ, whose call to conversion and service brings us together. We have lifted praise to God who is life, giving thanks for all God's gifts to us, especially for the life, death, and resurrection of Jesus Christ.

Now, trusting in God's unfailing mercy, we come to a time of confession. In confessing ourselves before God, we are keeping faith with one another and with God. We are examining our lives and exposing to the light of God's Word the breaches and breaks in our lives which we would rather overlook.

Confession is difficult for us, especially when we confess as a corporate body. We as individuals would rather not take responsibility for our ills as a Body. We are prepared to justify our personal thoughts and actions to God on our own.

The good news is that we do not have to justify ourselves. We can be fearless in confession, trusting that God will forgive us and remake us as servants of God's reign. This trust, this faith alone is granted to us by God as our justification (Romans 1:17).

Therefore we are freed and empowered to confess our corporate sins as well. We are enabled to face our failure to be an obedient church. We are given strength to shoulder one another's burdens and together seek God's healing.

A clear vision of what God intends the church to be and do today is possible only if we examine ourselves as a people set apart as God's own. Confession is risky, for it requires our willingness to give up old patterns and old assumptions that divide us from God and from one another.

But not to confess is to turn in upon ourselves, helpless to overcome that which hinders us from faithful discipleship. Our help is in the Lord. When we name our sins before God, we lay them at the mercy seat. God alone can remove them from us and free us for joyful obedience.

VITAL CONGREGATIONS—FAITHFUL DISCIPLES

Come, ye sinners, poor and needy,
weak and wounded, sick and sore;
Jesus ready stands to save you,
full of pity, love, and power.
I will arise and go to Jesus;
He will embrace me with his arms;
in the arms of my dear Savior,
O there are ten thousand charms.

Joseph Hart
The United Methodist Hymnal, No. 340

It's hard to deal with the question of when we feel most distant from God because it deals with the negative and that is something we normally do not want to do.

The Community Church
Morgantown, West Virginia

Merciful God,
we confess that we have not loved you with our whole heart.
We have failed to be an obedient church.
We have not done your will,
we have broken your law,
we have rebelled against your love,
we have not loved our neighbors,
and we have not heard the cry of the needy.
Forgive us, we pray.
Free us for joyful obedience,
through Jesus Christ our Lord.
Amen.

(From A Service of Word and Table I,
The United Methodist Hymnal, page 8)

The time has come for telling the truth about ourselves as United Methodist Christians. We need to give our sins a name. We love to gossip about ourselves, our fellow church members, our pastors, our annual conferences, our church business. We spend much time talking about ourselves, to ourselves. We are absorbed in ourselves.

But rarely do the words of our formal prayer of confession strike home: "We have failed to be an obedient church." We have failed. We do not speak the truth about ourselves before God, and thus are not obedient, that is, literally, able "to listen to" God's Word for us.

Turned inward, content to bemoan the state of our church, we do not face either the absolute judgment of God upon us, or the utterly astonishing forgiveness that God offers us. But unless we are truthful about giving our fears and failures a name, we cannot claim the mercies of the One who is the truth that makes us free.

We do not like to confess. Most of the time we reason that we are doing our best, that after all we are members of congregations and by serving the church we are surely serving Jesus. We go about our daily lives in the belief that as long as we are courteous and do no direct harm to another person, we are basically good. Thus we are free to pursue our own lifestyles and interests, limited only by what we can afford in time and money.

Confession puts all that at risk. To confess and ask for healing is also to ask God to change us, and change is frightening. To admit before God that our witness to the Kingdom flickers and dies, is also to ask God to give us courage to be more faithful servants; and service requires sacrifice.

But not to confess is to suffocate. The more we turn inward, the more we wither. The psalmist put it this way:

While I kept silence, my body wasted away
   through my groaning all day long.
For day and night your hand was heavy upon me;
   my strength was dried up as by the heat of summer.

Then I acknowledged my sin to you,
   and I did not hide my iniquity;
I said, "I will confess my transgressions to the LORD,"
   and you forgave the guilt of my sin.

(Psalm 32:3-5)

The United Methodist Church is the one on the stretcher (Mark 2). We are paralyzed by the loss of our culture's support. We have let our institutional structures become a burden to us.

Yet it is as though the ones who need us now—the poor, the oppressed, the sick, the estranged, the hopeless, the broken in spirit—have lifted us up and carried us to the Master.

And Jesus Christ even now is reaching out a hand to lift us off the mat. Christ is announcing to us: "Your sins are forgiven . . . Stand up and take your mat and walk" (Mark 2:9).

The decision is ours. What will we do? Will we be moved to walk with Christ into the hurts and hopes of this world? Or will we continue in our inertia?

Peter and Andrew, James and John only had to hear Jesus say, "Follow me," and they dropped their nets and went with him. They were ordinary people, but they followed and Jesus made them apostles of the gospel.

On the other hand, there was another man who came

When he returned to Capernaum after some days, it was reported that he was at home. So many gathered around that there was no longer room for them, not even in front of the door; and he was speaking the word to them. Then some people came, bringing to him a paralyzed man, carried by four of them. And when they could not bring him to Jesus because of the crowd, they removed the roof above him; and after having dug through it, they let down the mat on which the paralytic lay. When Jesus saw their faith, he said to the paralytic, "Son, your sins are forgiven." Now some of the scribes were sitting there, questioning in their hearts, "Why does this fellow speak in this way? It is blasphemy! Who can forgive sins but God alone?" At once Jesus perceived in his spirit that they were discussing these questions among themselves; and he said to them, "Why do you raise such questions in your hearts? Which is easier, to say to the paralytic, 'Your sins are forgiven,' or to say, 'Stand up and take your mat and walk'? But so that you may know that the Son of Man has authority on earth to forgive sins"—he said to the paralytic—"I say to you, stand up, take your mat and go to your home." And he stood up, and immediately took the mat and went out before all of them; so that they were all amazed and glorified God, saying, "We have never seen anything like this!"

Mark 2:1-12

VITAL CONGREGATIONS—FAITHFUL DISCIPLES

*Rock of Ages, cleft for me,
let me hide myself in thee;
let the water and the blood,
from thy wounded side which flowed,
be of sin the double cure;
save from wrath and make me pure.*

Augustus M. Toplady
The United Methodist Hymnal, No. 361

looking for Jesus to inquire about eternal life. He was a man of unquestioned faith and piety; he said his prayers, never missed services, put money in the offering plate. The only thing he lacked was companionship with Christ; but this he was unwilling to pursue, for he would have had to give up the preoccupations which kept him from Christ. Jesus said to him, "Follow me." But this man turned back (Mark 10:17-22).

Which one are we?

How can a church whose congregations collectively raise over two and a half billion dollars a year be immobilized by a sense of drift? Is it that our wealth of resources has turned us back from the joyful risk of discipleship?

Therefore let us confess our sins before God and one another. If we name them, speaking the truth in love, God has promised to forgive us and free us for new life in God's mercy and grace.

Let us confess before God our inertia as United Methodist Christians. We are very busy people. We are active in many causes. To an outsider we look like beehives of committee work and programs. But in our hearts we suffer emptiness and doubt. Busy with much serving, we know ourselves paralyzed by loss of contact with our Master, in whose company alone we find direction and purpose.

Like the scribes of the story in Mark 2, we do not see any connection between our paralysis and the forgiveness of our sins. We try all kinds of medicines to make us feel lively. We prioritize. We create new task forces. We demand better preachers. We look for a few quick and easy steps to rejuvenate our sense of mission. We buy computers to speed our work and adopt business techniques to help us organize our plans. We advertise, use mass mailing methods, produce television programs. But beneath all this activity, our painful lack of vision persists. The more aimless we feel, the more nostrums we take.

We have failed to be an obedient church. Forgive us, we pray. Free us for joyful obedience.

OUR CONFESSION AS A PEOPLE OF FAITH

Let us confess before God our preoccupation with church business. Working on church business has become our definition of discipleship. As willing volunteers we find ourselves discussing evangelism instead of inviting people to get to know the Lord, coordinating special offering Sundays instead of building houses for the poor. We equate church jobs with serving the Lord.

We use the term "full-time Christian service" to describe those whose salaries are paid by the local church or denomination. We think of ordained ministers as "professionals" who will do the church's work of "ministry" as a paid "vocation." We do not believe with conviction that all Christians, wherever they employ their talents, are in full-time Christian service. So we make little connection between our faith and the everyday world of home, factory, office, or school.

At the same time, we have become comfortable with hiring out our discipleship responsibilities. We give money to pay the salaries of those who will carry out ministry on our behalf. We enjoy the services of many able people, trained as experts in music, social work, education, and other fields. But to the extent that paid professionalism represents some few of us doing the work for all of us, it marks a failure in the discipleship that belongs to each of us.

We have developed a network of effective service agencies. We have raised money to support persons who devote themselves to working on critical problems of homelessness, poverty, and hunger. But seldom do most of us break bread with hungry people or sit in the homes of poor or unemployed families.

We have failed to be an obedient church. Forgive us, we pray. Free us for joyful obedience.

Let us confess before God that our conduct of church business makes us feel distant from God. We begin our meetings with routine prayer. We ask God to bless what we do without taking time to find out if God has any passion for the work we have chosen for ourselves. The leading of the Holy Spirit is vague to us; we are more comfortable with our bylaws and rules of order.

We feel most distant from God when, as individuals, committees or work areas, or as the church, we are inactive, complacent, or not focused, and when we are busy maintaining the organization or structure of the church (local or beyond) as an end in itself.
                                      Trinity Church
                                      Duncanville, Texas

VITAL CONGREGATIONS—FAITHFUL DISCIPLES

People appear to feel most distant from God when preparing, conducting, and attending meetings, when attending to administrative business of the church, and during Wednesday evening activities sessions when people appear less friendly.

First Church
Pensacola, Florida

*I sought the Lord, and afterward I knew
he moved my soul to seek him, seeking me.
It was not I that found, O Savior true;
no, I was found of thee.*

Anon.
The United Methodist Hymnal, No. 341

Having disposed of all possible "old business"—the agenda we carry over from the past—we turn at the last moment to "new business"—the arena in which God might have a chance of getting through to us. We save till last, when there is little time, the new challenges, the new visions of mission that might break us out of our inertia.

We pray that what we do might be God's will; but we have no sense of terror that God's will might be to overturn our church business. We know that God's will is fundamentally that the Kingdom come on earth. But just in case God is not prepared to act on that promise, or in case "the right hand of the Most High has changed" (Psalm 77:10), we are ready to go forward by the principles of market economics.

We measure the worth of our congregations by size and income, just as we judge people by the size of their homes and wealth of possessions. We value the numerical growth of our congregations, but our growth in faith we rarely discuss. We write "job descriptions" and "deploy personnel" to fill "positions" just like any other corporation or bureaucracy. The language of saints being given gifts by the Holy Spirit for the carrying out of Christ's ministry only decorates our established procedures, and so rings hollow and false.

Our management style is cut off from the wellsprings of our Wesleyan heritage. We design programs to attract people to our congregations, but give much less thought to how they can be invited into life with Christ. The disciplines of fasting, prayer, and visiting the sick, the poor, and those in prison, we find much too severe. We have trouble telling other people what makes a life Christlike, or worse, what difference it makes whether they are Christian or not.

Our personal experience of companionship with Christ grows cold. We glibly announce Jesus' presence with us, while assuming that he would, of course, be present whenever we choose. Meanwhile we neglect the sacraments in which Christ has promised his presence. We give little time to the meaning and interpretation of baptism. We conduct services of Holy Communion

OUR CONFESSION AS A PEOPLE OF FAITH

when we find it convenient, and then without the joyous sense of eating supper with our Lord.
We have failed to be an obedient church. Forgive us, we pray. Free us for joyful obedience.

Let us confess before God our nostalgia for the Protestant establishment, especially in North America. We long for "the good old days" when Protestant churches were full and community leaders attended them. We pine for the days when what was good for the nation was good for the church, and vice versa. We are not accustomed to the possibility that being a Christian might make us marginal people in our society.

For generations many of our congregations have been confirming the children of their own families, but far less frequently baptizing new Christians. We can see that we are getting older in both pew and pulpit. But we have neither the conviction nor the will to be apostles of the gospel among those who have not heard it, especially the young.

Our culture has eroded many of the old assumptions about belonging to a church. The question of why be a Christian or join a congregation is much sharper in this generation. We are not ready to respond to people who question the necessity of church membership. If belonging to a church is not just "the thing to do," then why really join? What is so compelling about Jesus Christ anyway?

We have been stunned by such questions. Most painfully, our own children have not been captivated by the Christian story. Our confirmation services have become "graduation ceremonies," as our children grow up to leave the church instead of finding their commitment and loyalty deepened.

We are less and less sure where our next generation of leadership will come from. We have been reluctant to challenge our own youth with the calling to Christian service. Much of our lay and clergy leadership is reaching retirement age. Our failure to call out and support candidates for ordained ministry forces us to count on the willingness of persons from other

The vast majority of worship services in which I have participated over the past decade or so have left me with the sense that what we are really doing is performing. Performing for one another—in the absence of any other reason to be there, in the absence of any Great Spectator, so to speak. The chancel has become a stage, the pulpit a lectern; the choir and organist offer programs, the minister gives a speech (preferably with as many one-liners as possible, and preferably short!); and the congregation is an audience, with "audience response" as in the other performances (TV) that seem to have set the pattern for all this.

It seems to me that I sense a loss. I feel deprived of anything approaching mystery. These middle class affairs that we conduct on Sunday mornings seem to me conspicuously devoid of awe.
Douglas John Hall, Professor
McGill University
Montreal, Canada

Our congregation is caring and sharing but we "shy away" from things that are controversial.
Wesley Chapel Church
Lincoln, Delaware

The United Methodist Church must be prepared for fundamental changes occurring in the world church. Christian population is growing most rapidly in Africa and Asia. There is a shift in the power of decision and in the vitality of church life. We live in a time of basic reordering of international Christianity. Christians on every continent will be receiving as well as sending missionaries and will be renewed by the strength of partnership and mutuality. New cultural influences are presenting themselves and calling us to enlarged world awareness. We are a part of a new, dynamic relationship, a relationship in which all of us will learn to listen as well as teach. Humility and gratitude must reshape our sense of mission responsibility.

Grace Upon Grace: The Mission Statement of The United Methodist Church

Now his elder son was in the field; and when he came and approached the house, he heard music and dancing. He called one of the slaves and asked what was going on. He replied, "Your brother has come, and your father has killed the fatted calf, because he has got him back safe and sound." Then he became angry and refused to go in . . . Then the father said to him, "Son, you are always with me, and all that is mine is yours. But we had to celebrate and rejoice, because this brother of yours was dead and has come to life; he was lost and has been found."

Luke 15:25-28, 31-32

Someone unkempt and untidy might feel uncomfortable here. On one occasion we had a wanderer come in. When he left mid-service, an usher followed to make sure he didn't "steal" something.

*College Place Church
Brunswick, Georgia*

"Lord, when was it that we saw you hungry or thirsty or a stranger or naked or sick or in prison, and did not take care of you?" Then he will answer them, "Truly I tell you, just as you did not do it to one of the least of these, you did not do it to me."

Matthew 25:44-45

A Black or other non-White person, or a poor person or someone poorly dressed might not feel comfortable here. Although there is a current of love and acceptance available, we have not found ways to express these qualities so that they are recognized by minorities.

*North Broadway Church
Columbus, Ohio*

denominations to accept appointments as United Methodist pastors.

Meanwhile, we watch with dismay as God continues to welcome home new people in congregations of other traditions. We grow skeptical of these new Christians, and criticize the denominations of which they are a part. As so-called "conservative" groups continue to expand, erecting new buildings and starting new ministries in our communities, we attack their message and talk foolishly of imitating their methods. They do not seem to appreciate our stature as established congregations of mature Christians. They also make us insecure in our own identity.

We suffer from "elder brother" syndrome. We are the brother who stayed home, loyally managing the household as we thought our parents wanted, while others were off squandering their fortunes. That we do not rejoice in God's growing family is the sinful fruit of our pride and preoccupation with our own social standing.

We have failed to be an obedient church. Forgive us, we pray. Free us for joyful obedience.

Let us confess before God our fear of others, of people not like ourselves. We look at the stranger; the homeless person; the person in clothing different from ours; the family of another language, culture, or race, and we see there our own fear of being strange and alone. We stay in the familiar places we have built for ourselves, and do our best to discourage outsiders from coming in. We want to worship with people like ourselves, who fit our stereotypes of family and citizenship.

Too few of our congregations are interracial. Too few include people from a variety of economic levels, especially the poor and unemployed. Unlike Abraham, we do not gladly entertain the sojourner in our house on the chance that she or he might be carrying a word from the Lord (Genesis 18:1-15). We are not prepared to receive the surprises or the insights that an outsider might offer us.

We have failed to be an obedient church. Forgive us, we pray. Free us for joyful obedience.

OUR CONFESSION AS A PEOPLE OF FAITH

Let us confess before God that we mirror the sins of the world more than we renounce them. The divisions and prejudices among the world's peoples are just as devastating in the church as in the larger society. Especially in North America, we are not willing to examine how the values that support our standard of living may affect other peoples.

We are "at home in Zion," certain that our prosperity and plenty are rewards from God for our being good people. We are content with our prejudice that if someone is poor, or far from home with no place to go, he or she must not have done those things that will gain God's favor.

Consequently, we are in no position to lead the nations to repentance either. Unwilling to receive the sojourner ourselves, we cannot condemn nations for uprooting and displacing refugees. Blind to the deadly effects of our consumption on the land, air, and water given us by a creating God, we cannot voice a warning about the impending disaster that awaits our earthly environment. Secure in our property, we will not protest massive expenditures on military arms that bankrupt the nations, or cry out against the readiness of nuclear missiles to destroy all of the life God created.

We have failed to be an obedient church. Forgive us, we pray. Free us for joyful obedience.

Let us confess before God that we are passive Christians. Forces are loose in the world that we do not understand or control. The gospel is not heard gladly as an answer to any "real" problems of humanity. So we withdraw into ourselves, content to let the good news of salvation be a private, internal, personal matter.

Our witness has grown pinched and narrow. We do not speak publicly of our faith. We do not have a witness for others of what Jesus Christ has done in our lives, or will do for the world. We do not invite even our friends to church. We do not take the opportunity of our friends' need to assure them of Christ's love.

We do not recognize ourselves as full human beings, creatures of God chosen and blessed with the potential to fulfill God's purposes for us. We lack faith that God

To respond faithfully it is necessary to confront our own unfaithfulness: unfaithfulness generated by bland, sentimental, comfortable, and blurred relating of the gospel to the world. We do not acknowledge the lost condition of the world, the radical alienation of people from God, or the depth of human hurt. We have too quickly bought the world's values, provided easy explanation, and excused the world or ourselves. But grace can also empower us to see the world from the standpoint of the gospel.

Grace Upon Grace: The Mission Statement of The United Methodist Church

O God, we enjoy being together. Forgive us when we enjoy that so much that we shut out others. Help us to welcome the strangers in our midst. And let us learn to love those children of yours who are different and welcome them into our fellowship.

Trinity Church
Lakewood, California

And to the angel of the church in Laodicea write: The words of the Amen, the faithful and true witness, the origin of God's creation:
"I know your works; you are neither cold nor hot. I wish that you were either cold or hot. So, because you are lukewarm, and neither cold nor hot, I am about to spit you out of my mouth."

Revelation 3:14-16

VITAL CONGREGATIONS—FAITHFUL DISCIPLES

*Softly and tenderly Jesus is calling,
calling for you and for me;
see, on the portals he's waiting and watching,
watching for you and for me.*

*O for the wonderful love he has promised,
promised for you and for me!
Though we have sinned, he has mercy and pardon,
pardon for you and for me.*

*Come home, come home;
you who are weary, come home;
earnestly, tenderly, Jesus is calling,
calling, O sinner, come home!*

Will L. Thompson
The United Methodist Hymnal, No. 348

*Come, all of you, come, men and women,
come forward, drink of the water provided for you;
all of you who are thirsty, come to me to drink
from the water of life, provided by Jesus your Lord.*

Laotian hymn;
trans. by Cher Lue Vang
The United Methodist Hymnal, No. 350

Lord, we confess that we have not reached out where all opportunities exist, and we are not giving fully of our time and talent as you would call us to serve You and Your church and Your kingdom.

The Church of Whitefish Bay
Whitefish Bay, Wisconsin

can use us. We do not believe that we have much of anything to give in the service of the Kingdom.

Our low self-esteem convinces us that there is really not much we can do to follow Jesus. Thus we absolve ourselves from growing into the discipleship we could have if only we put to work God's gifts to us.

We have failed to be an obedient church. Forgive us, we pray. Free us for joyful obedience.

Let us confess before God our spiritual emptiness. We do not know our own Scriptures. The words and images of the Bible are strange to us. We cannot find what we need, nor can we help others find their way into Scripture, because we do not know the Bible ourselves. Even our preaching is oddly unbiblical, as if the anecdotes of contemporary life were more inspiring than God's revelation in Scripture. The discipline of reading the Bible every day is as difficult for us as learning another language, and we are not persuaded of its usefulness.

We are hesitant to pray. In the words of John Wesley's covenant service, let us confess before God "the sterility and inconstancy of our prayers." We are afraid that if we really ask that God's will be done on earth, our lives can never be the same again. So we ask only for God's help in doing what we have already decided is the best thing for us.

We beg tamely for the things for which we ought to die. We pray for peace, but not for God to show us what to do for peace. We pray for a sick person's comfort, but are afraid to ask God to fulfill the kingdom promise of healing. We do not take time to meditate on the needs of others, so that we can intercede for them according to what they really need, and not what we casually think they need. We insulate ourselves from the real need of ourselves and our neighbor. We ask God to help us do what we have already determined to do, and to help our neighbor with what we have already decided is good for them. We do not throw ourselves on the mercy of God.

Isolated in our private lives, we do not sense that prayer overcomes our apathy and powerlessness by drawing us together as a spiritual community, in the

OUR CONFESSION AS A PEOPLE OF FAITH

presence of the one Lord. Hence we neglect to pray for one another as United Methodists, or for our conferences or leaders who embody our unity.

We have failed to be an obedient church. Forgive us, we pray. Free us for joyful obedience.

Let us confess before God that we are afraid to die. Many of our congregations are so caught up in trying to survive, that we have forgotten how to live. And the way to live is, as Jesus said, to risk death. We do not want to hear those words.

Determined to survive, we expend our energies maintaining our properties and our programs. Once a program has started, we cannot let it go even if the mission is more urgent elsewhere. We are moved to leave monuments to our discipleship, but not to die for it.

The fact that Jesus left no ruins, no monuments, no sanctuaries, threatens us. Determined to survive, we cannot really live in Christ's presence. For he is always moving on to the next town, to the next crowd of hungry listeners. We are left behind, not really trusting that if we went there, too, we might hear God's Word for us as well.

We have failed to be an obedient church. Forgive us, we pray. Free us for joyful obedience.

Let us confess before God that our inertia deadens our dreams. The onrushing changes and tensions of our world have made us numb. We choose to remain uninformed about critical issues that face the world: nuclear weapons, destruction of the environment, massive poverty. With stunted imaginations, we cannot put ourselves in the shoes of others, or begin to sense their plight.

We cannot envision what we could do to be effective witnesses to God's reign of love and justice. Without vision the people perish (Proverbs 29:18), and that is what we are slowly doing. For we do not share the biblical vision of a new humanity.

We have failed to be an obedient church. Forgive us, we pray. Free us for joyful obedience.

*Just as I am, though tossed about
with many a conflict, many a doubt,
fightings and fears, within, without,
O Lamb of God, I come, I come.*

Charlotte Elliott
The United Methodist Hymnal, No. 357

*Tú has venido a la orilla,
no has buscado ni a sabios ni a ricos,
tan sólo quieres que yo te siga.
Señor, me has mirado a los ojos
y sonriendo has dicho mi nombre;
en la arena he dejado mi barca;
junto a ti buscaré otro mar.*

Lord, you have come to the lakeshore
looking neither for wealthy nor wise ones;
you only asked me to follow humbly.
O Lord, with your eyes you have searched me
and while smiling have spoken my name;
now my boat's left on the shoreline behind me;
by your side I will seek other seas.

Cesareo Gabaraín;
trans. by Gertrude C. Suppe,
George Lockwood, and Raquel Gutiérrez-Achon
The United Methodist Hymnal, No. 344

© 1979, Cesareo Gabaraín. Published by OCP Publications, 5536 NE Hassalo, Portland, OR 97213. All rights reserved. Used with permission.

VITAL CONGREGATIONS—FAITHFUL DISCIPLES

Plenteous grace with thee is found,
grace to cover all my sin;
let the healing streams abound,
make and keep me pure within.
Thou of life the fountain art,
freely let me take of thee;
spring thou up within my heart;
rise to all eternity.

Charles Wesley
The United Methodist Hymnal, No. 479

We have failed to be an obedient church.

Therefore let us repent of "our manifold sins and wickedness, which we from time to time most grievously have committed," and turn to the Lord.

Let us examine our life together in congregations, and repent of that which divides us from our neighbor.

Let us examine our life as disciples, and repent of that which alienates us from Christ.

Let us examine the brokenness of the world, and repent of the ways we mirror that brokenness and ignore its pain.

Let us renounce all that stands between us and faithfulness to Jesus Christ.

Let us renounce our preoccupation with managing church business.

Let us renounce the prejudices that block our love of neighbor.

Let us renounce our nostalgia and fear.

Let us ask God's forgiveness and healing.

And Jesus Christ will heal us, forgive us, and set us free.

OUR FREEDOM IN CHRIST

Here is good news: in the name of Jesus Christ, our sins are forgiven. We are free to live a new life.

Our vision is cleared because the failings of the past are behind us. Mistakes and distortions from the past need no longer cloud our sight.

What we are beginning to see is that God's image in us shines through when we love as God loves. We are shaped by the image of the cross into communities of forgiveness and healing, where the Word of God's transforming love is visible in all that we do.

Therefore we are free to exchange the signs of peace that will reconcile us with one another. We are empowered to act as a sign of reconciliation in the brokenness of this world.

Here is good news.

**HEAR THE GOOD NEWS:
IN THE NAME OF JESUS CHRIST
WE ARE FORGIVEN.**

When we confess our sins, God is merciful and just, forgiving our sins and cleansing us from all unrighteousness (1 John 1:9).

**HEAR THE GOOD NEWS:
IN THE NAME OF JESUS CHRIST
WE ARE FORGIVEN.**

In the light of the cross, there is nothing that God will not forgive; for by the blood of Christ we are justified, and reconciled with God (Romans 5:9-10).

**HEAR THE GOOD NEWS:
IN THE NAME OF JESUS CHRIST
WE ARE FORGIVEN.**

Christ died for us while we were yet sinners; that proves God's love toward us (Romans 5:8). Our sins are beyond recompense, but God's mercy overflows for our salvation.

OUR FREEDOM IN CHRIST

**HEAR THE GOOD NEWS:
IN THE NAME OF JESUS CHRIST
WE ARE FORGIVEN.**

For freedom Christ has set us free (Galatians 5:1). Having renounced all that divides us from Christ and our neighbor, we are freed for joyful obedience.

**HEAR THE GOOD NEWS:
IN THE NAME OF JESUS CHRIST
WE ARE FORGIVEN.**

God wants to use our congregations for God's eternal purposes of saving the world. We are jars of clay indeed, bearing a treasure beyond all reckoning (2 Corinthians 4:7). God knows the cracks and weaknesses of our vessels; but God entrusts this precious mystery of salvation to us as stewards of the promise (1 Corinthians 4:1).

VITAL CONGREGATIONS—FAITHFUL DISCIPLES

Thanks be to thee, O Lord Jesus Christ, for all the benefits which thou hast given us; for all the pains and insults which thou hast borne for us. O most merciful Redeemer, friend, and brother, may we know thee more clearly, love thee more dearly, and follow thee more nearly, for thine own sake. Amen.
Richard of Chichester
The United Methodist Hymnal, No. 493

Here if nowhere else we may truly recognize ourselves in the picture of the disciples. All have abandoned. But this abandonment, denial, betrayal does not and cannot have the last word. At the end the lad in the tomb relays to the women a message from the one who was abandoned: "Go and tell Peter and the other disciples . . ." (Mark 16:7).

They have abandoned him. But they are still called disciples. Their betrayal is not the last word. And neither is ours. We may be terrible dunces about discipleship. So were they. We may be terrible cowards about what it costs. So were they. But they were still called to go back and start over. And so are we. They had a chance to try again and get it right. And so do we. And that Easter message scared them half to death. It scares me too.

Theodore W. Jennings, Jr.
Bakersfield, California

To live as a forgiven people, in the freedom of Christ, is to be "heirs of God and joint heirs with Christ." Therefore we "suffer with him so that we may also be glorified with him" (Romans 8:17). No longer slaves of sin but freed from our inertia, we are slaves of righteousness (Romans 6:16-18), bound to journey with Christ in this world. A risky, daring business it is, for it comes eventually to the foot of a cross.

Jesus suffered "outside the city gate in order to sanctify the people by his own blood" (Hebrews 13:12). By his sacrifice we are saved; by his blood we are forgiven; by his cross we are set free to serve. And to serve we must follow him outside the gate. No longer content to remain inside the city walls, comfortable, at ease in Zion, we are free to follow him into the promise of new life.

Therefore let us go to meet our Lord outside the gate. "For here we have no lasting city, but we are looking for the city that is to come" (Hebrews 13:13-14).

The time has come. This is the moment for us, as congregations and as disciples, to get up and walk.

Jesus is saying to us, your sins are forgiven. Stand up and take your mat and walk. Follow me now. Follow me into the lives of people looking desperately for meaning. Follow me into the homes of broken families. Follow me into the streets of drug dealers. Follow me into the barrios of people without homes or jobs. Follow me into the refugee camps of people displaced from their homeland. Follow me everywhere there are people who do not know the everlasting joy of God's salvation.

And there you will share my ministry of healing. You will break the bread of hope. You will announce forgiveness. You will proclaim God's saving grace in my name.

We may die there. But we will have new life because we are serving others. We will have new life because we are witnessing to the reign of God among real people with the real and biting problems of their lives.

Let us as a people forgiven and reconciled with God reach out in signs and gestures of peace and reconciliation with others.

Let us as vital congregations reach out in reconciliation with those excluded from our fellowship.

Let us as faithful disciples reach out in reconciliation with those from whom we are alienated.

Let us by God's grace be a sign of the wholeness and peace that mark Christ's new life in us.

HEARING THE WORD OF GOD

God whom we have gathered to praise, God with whom we have kept faith in confessing ourselves, God who forgives us and claims us as a people set apart: God has a Word for us today.

God's Word is life. Like water flowing in the wilderness, the Word bears for us the life-giving story of God's reaching toward us in unfailing love and persistent justice. In the Word we see God's vision of a world made whole.

The living water of God's Word comes to us through the stream of faithful witness across the centuries. The stream flows from Scripture. It flows from the mission of the early church. It flows through our heritage of faith, especially in the Wesleyan movement. And the stream of witness flows as well through our own congregations.

We hear God's Word for us today by listening carefully to this stream of witness. In hearing our foundational stories, we are refreshed and inspired for joining in God's mission.

As we hear these stories, we know that our initiative toward God, our response to what God has revealed to us, is already taking shape. Our calling sounds loud and clear from the Word. We must find our own place in the story, as faithful disciples gathered into vital congregations. For through our own acts of love and justice we may be instruments of God's grace in the world.

Then he brought me back to the entrance of the temple; there, water was flowing from below the threshold of the temple toward the east (for the temple faced east); and the water was flowing down from below the south end of the threshold of the temple, south of the altar. Then he brought me out by way of the north gate, and led me around on the outside to the outer gate that faces toward the east; and the water was coming out on the south side.

Going on eastward with a cord in his hand, the man measured one thousand cubits, and then led me through the water; and it was ankle-deep. Again he measured one thousand, and led me through the water; and it was knee-deep. Again he measured one thousand, and led me through the water; and it was up to the waist. Again he measured one thousand, and it was a river that I could not cross, for the water had risen; it was deep enough to swim in, a river that could not be crossed. He said to me, "Mortal, have you seen this?"

Then he led me back along the bank of the river. As I came back, I saw on the bank of the river a great many trees on the one side and on the other. He said to me, "This water flows toward the eastern region and goes down into the Arabah; and when it enters the sea, the sea of stagnant waters, the water will become fresh. Wherever the river goes, every living creature that swarms will live, and there will be very many fish, once these waters reach there. It will become fresh; and everything will live where the river goes. People will stand fishing beside the sea from Engedi to Eneglaim; it will be a place for the spreading of nets; its fish will be of a great many kinds, like the fish of the Great Sea. But its swamps and marshes will not become fresh; they are to be left for salt. On the banks, on both sides of the river, there will grow all kinds of trees for food. Their leaves will not wither nor their fruit fail, but they will bear fresh fruit every month, because the water for them flows from the sanctuary. Their fruit will be for food, and their leaves for healing."

Ezekiel 47:1-12

Very truly, I tell you, no one can enter the kingdom of God without being born of water and Spirit. (John 3:5)

Those who drink of the water that I will give them will never be thirsty. The water that I will give will become in them a spring of water gushing up to eternal life. (John 4:14)

When the prophet Ezekiel envisioned the return of the people Israel to the Holy City from exile in Babylon, he pictured a stream welling up from the threshold of the Temple. For God was there, purifying and sustaining the people chosen to be faithful to God's purposes in the world. As the stream flowed out and became a river of fresh, life-giving water, it nourished trees of every kind. The trees bore fruit in all seasons, for this was God's land; and their leaves gave healing to anyone who touched them (Ezekiel 47:1-12).

Wherever the people of God gather in the name of Jesus Christ, there is a wellspring of this living water. There is a stream of life flowing from the threshold of the house of God. And joined with the streams from many congregations, it gathers into a knee-deep confluence, and into a neck-deep river, and finally into a torrent of joy.

"There is a river whose streams make glad the city of God" (Psalm 46:4). It flows "bright as crystal ... through the middle of the street of the city" (Revelation 22:1-2). It sweeps along, taking before it everything that stands in the way of the reign of God. In the city of our God, "justice roll[s] down like waters, / and righteousness like an everflowing stream" (Amos 5:24).

By the waters of this river, Christ's disciples are cleansed and set apart as members of the family of God. In their baptism they die with Christ and rise with him, born anew into life in the Spirit. They are claimed and bound for the city of God, where justice and integrity flow.

Like the trees planted by this flowing stream, vital congregations grow up into fullness of life. Rooted in the promise of the resurrection, nourished by Christ's presence, vital congregations offer strength and courage to all who pass under their influence.

Vital congregations produce the fruit of healing and peace: disciples who are alive with the love of Christ and faithful to Christ's ministry and mission. Through vital congregations, those who would be disciples of Christ are nurtured in the paths that lead to life (Psalm 16:11). They are provided the gifts to be witnesses and servants of the kingdom of God.

What makes a Christian congregation vital is its life in Christ. Its vitality is fed by the springs of Christ's healing, forgiveness, and hope. Born of water and the Spirit, the congregation is a vessel washed clean and filled by the Spirit with gifts of life.

In seeking vision for the church, we are tempted to work at institutional measures first. But programs, attendance figures, and budgets have meaning only as expressions of discipleship sustained by life in Christ. What must feed our vision is the spring of Christ. The life and work of our congregations bears fruit for the reign of God to the extent that we draw our life from Christ.

The Samaritan woman at Jacob's well asked Jesus where she could get the living water of which he was telling her. He replied that the water he gave her would become an inner spring, welling up into eternal life. "Sir," she pleaded, "give me this water, so that I may never be thirsty" (John 4:5-15).

We find ourselves today with the same need and the same question. We need this living water. We thirst to find out where to get it.

One of the ways God's stream of living water is available to us is through the river of witness that flows from Scripture through Christian history and into the life of our congregations. When we listen for God's Word to us as United Methodist Christians, we find ourselves rehearsing the stories in which we are deeply rooted.

We recall and relive the story of Jesus, who came to announce God's reign, to show us a way of life that gives glory to God, and to die for our salvation.

*Shall we gather at the river,
where bright angel feet have trod,
with its crystal tide forever
flowing by the throne of God?*

*Yes, we'll gather at the river,
the beautiful, the beautiful river,
gather with the saints at the river
that flows by the throne of God.*

Robert Lowry
The United Methodist Hymnal, No. 723

So he came to a Samaritan city, called Sychar, near the plot of ground that Jacob had given to his son Joseph. Jacob's well was there, and Jesus, tired out by his journey, was sitting by the well. It was about noon.

A Samaritan woman came to draw water, and Jesus said to her, "Give me a drink." (His disciples had gone to the city to buy food.) The Samaritan woman said to him, "How is it that you, a Jew, ask a drink of me, a woman of Samaria?" (Jews do not share things in common with Samaritans.) Jesus answered her, "If you knew the gift of God, and who it is that is saying to you, 'Give me a drink,' you would have asked him, and he would have given you living water." The woman said to him, "Sir, you have no bucket, and the well is deep. Where do you get that living water? Are you greater than our ancestor Jacob, who gave us the well, and with his sons and his flocks drank from it?" Jesus said to her, "Everyone who drinks of this water will be thirsty again, but those who drink of the water that I will give them will never be thirsty. The water that I will give will become in them a spring of water gushing up to eternal life." The woman said to him, "Sir, give me this water, so that I may never be thirsty or have to keep coming here to draw water."

John 4:5-15

VITAL CONGREGATIONS—FAITHFUL DISCIPLES

We had purchased a Jewish synagogue and are using it as our church building. The beautiful sanctuary stained glass windows are decorated with Jewish symbols. A few years ago, we decorated the remaining windows in the sanctuary with Jesus' image as the good shepherd in stained glass. The sanctuary seems to be the most wondrous place to worship God. It is also a very meaningful place to signify our journey from the Hebrew tradition and the Protestant tradition, finally to that of Korean-American.

First Korean Church
Chicago, Illinois

United Methodists share with other Christians the conviction that Scripture is the primary source and criterion for Christian doctrine. Through Scripture the living Christ meets us in the experience of redeeming grace. We are convinced that Jesus Christ is the living Word of God in our midst whom we trust in life and death.

"Our Theological Task,"
The Book of Discipline, 1988, ¶69

We celebrate the action of the Holy Spirit in creating and building up the church.

We call to mind the nature and purpose of the church that has characterized it from the beginning in New Testament times.

We tell again the story of John Wesley and the unique mission of Methodism that has emerged over 250 years.

Finally, we recall with warmth and appreciation the stories of our own congregations and their witness over the years. We remember the saints who have gone before us in the faith, and who have brought us into the presence of God.

Tracing our roots through the rich soil of Scripture and history leads us back to the springs from which our life has come. It freshens those springs for our life as congregations tomorrow. To our foundational stories we now turn.

Living by the Story of Jesus

Whoever believes in me believes not in me but in him who sent me. And whoever sees me sees him who sent me. I have come as light into the world, so that everyone who believes in me should not remain in the darkness. (John 12:44-46)

Christian congregations are called into being by the first words of Jesus recorded in the Gospel of Mark: "The time is fulfilled, and the kingdom of God has come near; repent, and believe in the good news" (1:15). This was the announcement that changed the world, and is echoed in the witness of congregations today.

Jesus called his hearers to repentance and conversion. Conversion means a complete turning around, or upside down, a whole new way of seeing. In repentance those who hear and respond to Jesus Christ are turning away from the life of the past and living in a new time.

To such a turnaround Jesus called all who had ears to hear and eyes to see. For only by seeing things upside down or in reverse would the people catch a glimpse of the reign of God. "He has brought down the powerful

HEARING THE WORD OF GOD

from their thrones, / and lifted up the lowly," sang Mary of Jesus' birth (Luke 1:52). The tiniest mustard seed becomes a luxuriant bush where birds can nest, said Jesus. The kingdom of God is like the woman who swept out her entire house to find a single coin. The blind see, the lame walk, the poor have good news preached to them. Everything is the opposite of the world's normal expectations.

Jesus gave plentiful signs of what life in God's reign is like. To the paralyzed he said, take up your pallet and walk. To the blind he said, have your sight, and go home to serve God among your people. With the hungry he broke bread for all to have enough and to spare. He cast out the demons that kept people from fullness of life. By such signs he showed that God's reign is a time of wholeness, fulfillment, and justice.

According to Mark, no sooner had Jesus preached the gospel of the coming reign of God than he began to say to certain people, "Follow me." And so they left the fishing net, the tax office, the home town, and went off to follow.

One of the remarkable silences of the Bible is the almost total lack of information about those followers. We have only their names, but nothing about their families, their stories, their character. The effect of this is profound. The followers of Jesus could have been anyone. No special need, qualification, or desire was necessary. And because these followers had no particular face in the Gospels, it is possible for every believer to imagine his or her own face in the company of Jesus.

They came to be called disciples, those who learn as understudies of their master. But unlike other disciples these did not seek their teacher; he sought them out. Moreover he did not teach a set body of principles or rules. He asked them to follow him wherever the road might lead.

Jesus was a teacher who knew the law of Moses and interpreted it for his times. But he taught by deed as well as word, calling not students, but followers who would learn to imitate his actions.

Thus the disciples found Jesus' personal presence

My soul proclaims the greatness of the Lord,
my spirit rejoices in God my Savior,
  who has looked with favor on me, a lowly servant.
From this day all generations shall call me blessed:
the Almighty has done great things for me
  and holy is the name of the Lord,
  whose mercy is on those who fear God
  from generation to generation.
The arm of the Lord is strong,
  and has scattered the proud in their conceit.
God has cast down the mighty from their thrones
  and lifted up the lowly.
God has filled the hungry with good things
  and sent the rich empty away.
God has come to the aid of Israel, the chosen servant,
  remembering the promise of mercy,
  the promise made to our forebears,
  to Abraham and his children for ever.

The *Magnificat*, Luke 1:46b-55
The United Methodist Hymnal, No. 199

English translation of Canticle of Mary by the International Consultation on English Texts.

The greatest symbol we have in our church is a twenty-foot tall colored stone window of Jesus Christ. Some see in that picture an ascending Christ who takes his beloved children with him. Others, seeing his outstretched palms, see a welcoming Christ who welcomes all persons, and makes us an inclusive church in our community. Others see the outstretched arms as a way of saying, "Come unto me all who labor and are heavy laden, and I will give you rest." We are a united church, symbolized by a banner telling of the time the United Church of Christ and the Methodist Church here decided to come under one roof and work together to serve Christ and this community.

The United Church of Faulkton
Seneca United Methodist Church
Faulkton, South Dakota

VITAL CONGREGATIONS—FAITHFUL DISCIPLES

Disciples attach themselves to a teacher who will teach them how to live. They are not there to learn math or physics or theology but life.

Theodore W. Jennings, Jr.
Bakersfield, California

A vital congregation is involved in development projects and has a caring love for people. You will never find a vital congregation that does not care for the poor. This congregation has strong programs for women, work, alphabetization (literacy-education), home visitation, and personal evangelism, caring for those who are in need.

The United Methodist Church
Nyabugoga-Gitega, Burundi

One week before her death, a member of the congregation was wheeled to the front of the sanctuary by her husband at the conclusion of a Sunday morning worship service. Sitting in her wheelchair she spoke extemporaneously of her faith and joy in Christ. Such a public statement was decidedly "out of character" for her. We recall the sacredness of the moment: her genuine expression of emotion shared with an accepting, affirming group of people called together in Christ's name. The freedom, joy, and pain of this moment left an indelible impression on those who witnessed it.

West Nash Church
Wilson, North Carolina

At one Christmas Eve candlelight service, two of our older members were standing up at the altar with their candles since they were unable to process out by the fountain. It was like a glimpse of eternity.

Wynnton Church
Columbus, Georgia

deeply compelling. They followed him simply to enjoy fellowship with the Son of God.

Having begun to show them what God's reign is like, Jesus sent his followers out, giving them authority to do likewise. The apostles (literally "those sent as messengers") were given power to cast out demons, heal the sick, and announce the good news of repentance, conversion, and the coming of the reign of God (Matthew 10; Mark 6:7-13).

But this was only the first stage of the apostolate. When Jesus appeared after his resurrection, he again gave the disciples authority, this time to go into all the world and make disciples. He charged them with teaching people "to obey everything that I have commanded you" (Matthew 28: 16-20). Love of God and love of neighbor were the foremost commandments. The apostles were to demonstrate in their own lives how these twin loves could be the foundation of a transformed world.

In every word and deed Jesus showed what God is like and what the promise of God's reign holds for us. But nowhere did he make this more vivid or more compelling than at the cross.

At the cross, he took his walk with those who suffer a final step, even to death, standing with them as redeeming Lord. At the cross, he took his promise of God's love and justice a final step, even to death, showing that suffering for the kingdom is redemptive and that God is not afraid to risk everything for the salvation of the world.

For God was in Christ reconciling an alienated and sinful world to God. Our faith in him "who was handed over to death for our trespasses and was raised for our justification" is "reckoned to us as righteousness" (Romans 4:22-25). Through Christ the burden of our sinfulness is lifted, and we are freed for the obedience of the cross.

Yet even the bondage of death, what seems to be the final answer to life, cannot hold Christ. In the eternal power of God Christ has risen again, the first fruit of the harvest of God's new creation.

HEARING THE WORD OF GOD

The Resurrection is a foretaste of God's ultimate plan for the transformation of the world. In the risen Christ is hope for the final conquering of sin and death. Through the Resurrection our hope embraces all the world in every age. For in the fullness of time, everything will be gathered up into Christ, "things in heaven and things on earth" (Ephesians 1:10).

In the risen Christ, all who have followed Jesus to the cross are chosen and freed to "live for the praise of his glory" (Ephesians 1:12) Through the power of the Resurrection, all congregations are given courage to embrace the whole inhabited earth, the *oikoumene*, the household of earth, with signs of hope. For by God's action, "every knee should bend . . . / and every tongue should confess that Jesus Christ is Lord, / to the glory of God the Father" (Philippians 2:10-11).

Christian congregations are gatherings of ordinary people, complete with all our hungers, needs and longings, who have heard, however faintly, the compelling voice of this story. We are converted, converting, and hoping yet to be converted. We are seeking God's grace to turn our lives around, and the love of Christ to help us live by the values of the Kingdom.

As apostles of this gospel, we cannot help but give witness to others of our new life in Christ. We seek to carry on Christ's ministry of reconciling love by giving signs of healing and comfort. We feed the hungry and give shelter to those who have no home simply as a response to Jesus' own life and witness.

Our congregations are called into fellowship with Christ. And if we follow him into the places he went, into the hurts, hungers, and happiness of life, we will surely find Christ there.

Indeed, as we are shaped by the gospel story, we are called to take up the cross. Under its weight we find courage for living in Christ's way. In its shadow we find "a home within the wilderness" that conquers our fear of death. We become fearless people, living in the knowledge that God's reign has already begun, unshakable in our faith that Christ will come again to rule the earth.

Christ is risen! Shout Hosanna!
Celebrate this day of days.
Christ is risen! Hush in wonder;
all creation is amazed.
In the desert all-surrounding,
see, a spreading tree has grown.
Healing leaves of grace abounding
bring a taste of love unknown.

Brian Wren
The United Methodist Hymnal, No. 307
Hope Publishing Co.; 380 S. Main Pl.; Carol Stream, IL 60188.

Windows at the top of the sanctuary bring in the sun and pull worshipers' eyes up, into the heavens. They make visible unexpected signs of God—birds, clouds, rain, lightning. Banners and altar cloths brighten worship and give a good sense of the church season. Everything in the sanctuary is moveable as the Spirit and needs of the time dictate. The chairs are arranged in a U-shaped, almost circular formation so people can see each other and can easily tell if someone has a need or concern.

Middletown Church
Middletown, Maryland

We are thankful for those who are strong in their faith and for the examples they lead. We thank you, God, for the continued acceptance of all peoples seeking You at Park Street. Help us in understanding and accepting others who are different. Let us see the good in them as your Children as well as ourselves.

We ask for guidance for Park Street to be of service to the city. Help families with personal and addiction problems that are not attending now. Be with us as a congregation that we may minister to the community as you would have us do.

Park Street Church
Atlanta, Georgia

VITAL CONGREGATIONS—FAITHFUL DISCIPLES

The gifts we bring include an abiding concern for both local and global mission work, multi-talented people who share their gifts graciously and generously, the ability to work together for goals we have set, and the acceptance of the participation of all ages and conditions of persons—there is no generation gap here.

Oakdale Church
Grand Rapids, Michigan

*Like the murmur of the dove's song,
like the challenge of her flight,
like the vigor of the wind's rush,
like the new flame's eager might:
Come, Holy Spirit, come.*

*To the members of Christ's body,
to the branches of the Vine,
to the church in faith assembled,
to her midst as gift and sign:
Come, Holy Spirit, come.*

Carl P. Daw, Jr.
The United Methodist Hymnal, No. 544
Hope Publishing Co.; 380 S. Main Pl.; Carol Stream, IL 60188.

We have many gifts. We have five medical doctors and the skills that they bring. We have many school teachers, active and retired, and school administrators and their skills. We have several top agricultural scientists with Ph.D. degrees, who help farmers every day by providing information about animal feeds, grasses, milk protein, etc. We have several artists, lawyers, a judge, a retired mayor.

Centenary Church
Franklinton, Louisiana

Some months ago, our lay leader said he was tired of coming to church every Sunday and being greeted by someone needing change for coffee. So we started serving coffee and now have nearly 100 street people coming for coffee, donuts, a song service and Sunday School class. Five elderly people who have always

Living by the Power of the Holy Spirit

I have said these things to you while I am still with you. But the Advocate, the Holy Spirit, whom the Father will send in my name, will teach you everything, and remind you of all that I have said to you. (John 14:25-26)

When Jesus commissioned his disciples to carry on his ministry and mission, he promised them an Advocate, the Holy Spirit, who would also come from God. Although Christ would not be with them in the flesh, they would be empowered to act in his name by the Holy Spirit. Indeed, the Spirit's coming inspired the beginning of the church.

Christian congregations "born of water and the Spirit" are fed by the living water of Christ and enlivened by the breath of the Spirit. Congregations are called out, formed, gifted, and empowered by the Holy Spirit. For the Spirit, in Greek the *pneuma* or air, is the wind that blows fresh and pure, making all things new.

With a sound like a mighty wind, the Holy Spirit blew life into the church in an upper room in Jerusalem (Acts 2). Gathered there was a little group of men and women who had walked with Jesus and witnessed the risen Christ. But they were cautious and afraid, unsure what their next steps should be. Could ordinary people like them really become messengers of the good news Jesus had preached? Why would anyone look or listen to them for a vision from the Lord?

By the wind of the Spirit they found their voice. Anointed by dancing flames they received the gift of speaking in every language under the sun. All the nations could now hear them gladly.

They were given courage to proclaim the good news of hope. They were given the words they needed to say what they believed and to persuade others to put their trust in Christ as well.

The Spirit confirmed their calling to continue Christ's ministry, healing the sick, binding up the broken-hearted. And by the Spirit they were united in a covenant community that was itself a sign of the reign of God.

Together they would break bread and pray, "sell their possessions and goods and distribute the proceeds to all, as any had need" (Acts 2:45). They were a fellowship of hospitality, their table open to all who sought the bread of life.

The Holy Spirit baptizes disciples of Christ to form such congregations today. By the Spirit ordinary people find voice and courage to say and do what they never thought possible. With purifying flame the Spirit bestows the gifts with which disciples can witness to God's coming reign.

In the materialistic culture that dominates the world today, dividing rich from poor and identifying the abundant life with possessions, the first congregation formed by the Holy Spirit seems utopian. We lack the courage and will to live in such a way.

But the Spirit has not lost its power to create. The Spirit moved across the waters at creation, bringing earth to life. The Spirit blew through the upper room in Jerusalem to bring into being out of modest materials, a church that would carry on Christ's ministry.

By the power of the Holy Spirit our congregations can preach redemption in Christ. We can demonstrate the joy, daring, and peace that come from following Christ wherever he leads. The Spirit stirs us from our lethargy. The Spirit gives us our voice, and sets us on fire to proclaim the good news of the coming of the Lord.

The Holy Spirit bestows gifts with which disciples can serve the Lord, and creates communities within which those gifts can be nurtured and empowered. In the congregation some are called and gifted to be teachers, tellers of the story of God's incarnate love. Some are called to be prophets, by faith confronting the lack of integrity and justice in everyday life. Some are apostles gifted as ambassadors for Christ's message of forgiveness and reconciliation. Some are called into the service of feeding the hungry, sheltering the homeless, helping the powerless. (See 1 Corinthians 12 and Ephesians 4.)

But this is not an exhaustive list. The gifts of the people of God are as various as the people themselves. Some have the gift of organizing, some of visiting with strangers, some of designing artwork. Some people

used the International Lesson Series share their teacher and join these street people for their lesson.
Snyder Memorial Church
Jacksonville, Florida

Our members are highly educated in various fields and bring different talents to our church, including music, engineering, architecture, and economics. Those with bilingual capabilities are increasing in number and should be more fully utilized for creative programming in the future.
Korean Church of Ann Arbor
Ann Arbor, Michigan

O Great Spirit,
  whose breath gives life to the world,
  and whose voice is heard in the soft breeze:
We need your strength and wisdom.
Cause us to walk in beauty. Give us eyes
  ever to behold the red and purple sunset.
Make us wise so that we may understand
  what you have taught us.
Help us learn the lessons you have hidden
  in every leaf and rock.
Make us always ready to come to you
  with clean hands and steady eyes,
so when life fades, like the fading sunset,
  our spirits may come to you without shame. Amen.
Trad. Native American prayer
The United Methodist Hymnal, No. 329

For this reason I remind you to rekindle the gift of God that is within you through the laying on of my hands; for God did not give us a spirit of cowardice, but rather a spirit of power and of love and of self-discipline.

Do not be ashamed, then, of the testimony about our Lord or of me his prisoner, but join with me in suffering for the gospel, relying on the power of God.
2 Timothy 1:6-8

VITAL CONGREGATIONS—FAITHFUL DISCIPLES

But each of us was given grace according to the measure of Christ's gift. . . .
The gifts he gave were that some would be apostles, some prophets, some evangelists, some pastors and teachers, to equip the saints for the work of ministry, for building up the body of Christ, until all of us come to the unity of the faith and of the knowledge of the Son of God, to maturity, to the measure of the full stature of Christ. We must no longer be children, tossed to and fro and blown about by every wind of doctrine, by people's trickery, by their craftiness in deceitful scheming. But speaking the truth in love, we must grow up in every way into him who is the head, into Christ, from whom the whole body, joined and knit together by every ligament with which it is equipped, as each part is working properly, promotes the body's growth in building itself up in love.
Ephesians 4:7, 11-16

Christ is made the sure foundation,
Christ the head and cornerstone;
chosen of the Lord and precious,
binding all the church in one;
holy Zion's help forever,
and her confidence alone.
7th cent. Latin;
trans. by John Mason Neale
The United Methodist Hymnal, No. 559

One man has arthritis and finds it difficult to sit in worship and rarely attends, yet prepares marvelous works of art to be used in worship each week.
Oak Grove Church
Jackson, Tennessee

We have members with varied religious experiences, many with organizational and leadership abilities. Members are gifted with a variety of abilities in: music, speaking, clerical work, culinary activity, craft-making, sewing, carpentry, and art. We have a growing number of senior citizens with time and know how to compose a letter, or when to give a child an encouraging hug, or when to speak a word of judgment to help another person see herself as others see her. "We have gifts that differ according to the grace given to us," wrote Paul, but we all "are one body in Christ, and individually we are members one of another" (Romans 12:5-6).

There are many callings, many gifts. Every congregation is given life by the multiple gifts of the Spirit. Indeed by the Spirit, disciples are given whatever they need to be in ministry in Christ's name. For the Spirit does not leave the faithful without power to do what Christ commands.

By the power of the Holy Spirit, disciples are built up (in Greek, *oiko-dome*) into one household (*oikos*) of faith. Set close to Christ, the chief cornerstone, faithful disciples become "living stones." Gathered into vital congregations they make up a "spiritual house" where God lives (1 Peter 2:4-5; Ephesians 2:22). The Greek *oikos pneumatikos* (1 Peter 2:5), house of wind, suggests a household through which the fresh air of the Spirit continually blows, bringing newness of life.

Every disciple is different; each is like a stone with a peculiar shape and size and its own oddities. But aligned on Christ these stones make up a house of service to the Lord. Each has a place and a role to play. Fitted together like stones in a wall, equipped for exercising their gifts, disciples make a unity in the work of ministry (Ephesians 4:12).

Each disciple is a steward (in Greek, *oiko-nomoi*, household manager) of her or his own gift. That is, each one is responsible for the grace given by God, and for putting that particular talent, skill, or trait to work in the service of others (1 Peter 4:10).

This is the vocation or calling that all Christians share: not their vocation in the limited sense of how they "make a living," but their calling to be stewards of the mercies of God. "You were called to the one hope of your calling" (Ephesians 4:4): the hope of Christ who in God's plan or "economy" of salvation will come again to reign in God's kingdom (Ephesians 1:9-10).

Faithful disciples live by the promises of God's

economy (in Greek, *oikonomia*, household management). In God's economy manna falls plentifully in the wilderness, water springs from desert rocks, whole bottles of perfume are poured out as a gesture of God's overflowing grace and forgiveness (Mark 14:3-9), bread is broken out for thousands from but five loaves (John 6:1-15). In God's economy no one is hungry, for there is plenty for all when everyone shares what they have. No one is burdened with poverty or want, for each one lives in dignity.

Faithful disciples believe that God provides what is needed for each day, and that therefore there is no need to hoard, to "store up into barns," or to bury one's talents in order to save them. From their own family household *(oikos)*, to the household of faith *(oikos pneumatikos)*, to the whole household of earth *(oikoumene)*, disciples serve as stewards of God's economy *(oikonomia)*. They are not bound to the economics of buying and owning more things, but to "the riches of [God's] grace that he lavished on us" (Ephesians 1:8). Congregations formed by the Holy Spirit announce that God plans to refashion the world into a new creation with Christ uniting all in all, and for that time Christians live. In this ecumenical hope, disciples are united with Christians everywhere, one in faith and one in service to the whole household of earth. In this liberating hope, disciples are freed from the slavery of the flesh to enjoy the fruits of the Spirit: "love, joy, peace, patience, kindness, generosity, faithfulness, gentleness, and self-control" (Galatians 5:22-23). For the Spirit is life.

Living by the Witness of the New Testament Church

He said to them, "But who do you say that I am?" Simon Peter answered, "You are the Messiah, the Son of the living God." And Jesus answered him, "Blessed are you, Simon son of Jonah! For flesh and blood has not revealed this to you, but my Father in heaven. And I tell you, you are Peter, and on this rock I will build my church, and the gates of

expertise and a large supply of younger people in the community with good ideas and untapped resources.
Federalsburg-Denton Charge
Federalsburg, Maryland

At the back of the church, we have restored the 1940 stained glass windows from the United Brethren Church. We dedicated them to a former E.U.B. member. He was a lifetime treasurer for the church and kept books that did more than report figures— they told stories. He would not just write: Groceries $10. He would write in his book: "We spent $10 for food for the Sunday School picnic where 37 attended and Mrs. Harrison read poetry."
The Church of St. Thomas
St. Thomas, Pennsylvania

*All praise to our redeeming Lord,
who joins us by his grace,
and bids us, each to each restored,
together seek his face.*

*He bids us build each other up;
and, gathered into one,
to our high calling's glorious hope
we hand in hand go on.*
Charles Wesley
The United Methodist Hymnal, No. 554

As a new congregation less than three years old, we do not have a permanent worship building. Rented space is "converted" each Sunday into "holy space." Thus our feeling about worship space is more related to people than objects. This is not perceived by the congregation as a problem, rather, a blessing.

VITAL CONGREGATIONS—FAITHFUL DISCIPLES

In the absence of "sense," we sense a genuine spirit of worship. A sense of flexibility exists in the less formal setting along with a strong ritual using the Word and Table structure each week with or without communion. One person mentioned that the "noise" of a non-worship site causes us to work harder at sensing the presence of God; and we accomplish that. Another important sense is of people—real live flesh—as we pass the peace each week. It sometimes seems as if the "peace" is getting out of hand; then again, what's wrong with that!

Resurrection Church
Durham, North Carolina

United Methodist work in the Cordillera Area in Northern Philippines was begun in 1960 by eight Methodists and a missionary Filipino pastor who was sent to survey the place. In that same year, the First Methodist Church in Baguio City was organized. Using as a sanctuary an old discarded army quonset hut, the church today has a membership of close to 500 with many students, a beautiful new house of worship, and an outreach program covering the large mountain areas of northern Luzon. It now supports three smaller, growing churches.

*I am the church! You are the church!
We are the church together!
All who follow Jesus, all around the world!
Yes, we're the church together!*

Richard K. Avery and Donald S. Marsh
The United Methodist Hymnal, No. 558

Hope Publishing Co.; 380 S. Main Pl.; Carol Stream, IL 60188.

Our stories are not of objects but of people. We all agree that the community would not be the same without our church. (We are the only mainline de-

Hades will not prevail against it. (Matthew 16:15-18)

Paul, called to be an apostle of Christ Jesus by the will of God, and our brother Sosthenes, to the church of God that is in Corinth, to those who are sanctified in Christ Jesus, called to be saints, together with all those who in every place call on the name of our Lord Jesus Christ, both their Lord and ours: Grace to you and peace from God our Father and the Lord Jesus Christ. (1 Corinthians 1:1-3)

Within a generation of Jesus' death and resurrection, the faithful were gathering regularly in assemblies of witness and service. They met on Sundays to rehearse the story of Jesus and remember his resurrection "on the first day of the week." They sang and prayed, for one another and for the return of their Lord. They told one another what they knew of Jesus, and shared a meal together as he had taught the first disciples to do. They took a collection so that they could care for the poor.

The story of the early church has provided enduring springs of congregational vitality across the centuries. Every period of reformation in the church's history has been inspired by congregational life as it is described especially in the New Testament letters. The church today is entering into such a reformation period again, as congregations spring up in many lands and cultures, and as established congregations seek new life and mission for the century ahead.

The emerging world culture of the twenty-first century is much like the culture of the ancient Mediterranean world. Religions of many varieties meet and mix, sometimes clashing, sometimes blending into a muddled stew of beliefs. ***Contemporary Christians have inherited the same task that confronted the first Christians. We must continually learn what is distinctive about our faith, and take courage to practice it.***

The Church as Local and Universal

The first assemblies of the faithful followers of Jesus Christ came to be called by the name *ecclesia*, the root of words like ecclesiastical or the Spanish *iglesia*. While the word means simply "church" to modern people, its original sense is important. In the centuries before Christ, *ecclesia* was a Greek term for the town meeting of free male citizens. It described a public gathering in which the male citizenry were called together to discuss the common good of the city.

Ecclesia was related to the Greek word for "call." Christians may have liked it because it suggested that they had been called together by their Lord. Perhaps also they preferred it for its sense of openness to the public, although Christians drew no boundaries around their new "public" at all. They were as likely to be women as men, to be Gentiles or Jews, slave or free, rich or poor.

For the apostle Paul the *ecclesia* meant both the local meeting of the people of faith in each town or village, and their larger place in the universal people who follow Christ. He did not want any local gathering to lose its sense of being part of a larger movement. At the same time, the larger movement of Christianity had no real meaning apart from actual witnessing assemblies of Christians in particular places.

Thus the ecclesia, the church of Jesus Christ, is both local and universal at the same time. There is no abstract, universal Christian faith without actual gatherings of Christians in particular places. At the same time, there is no local meeting in the name of Christ that is not given life by the same Spirit who builds up the church wherever the gospel is proclaimed.

Our various local congregations are united with Christian congregations down the street and around the world, whether their name is Baptist, Roman Catholic, Greek Orthodox, Presbyterian, or United Methodist. We all receive the same promise of the good news. We all enjoy the same Holy Spirit bestowing the gifts we need for mission and ministry. There is "one Lord, one faith, one baptism" (Ephesians 4:5), and our assemblies are joined in a common chorus of worship, song, and prayer that embraces the earth.

Each congregation is a peculiar mix of the universal and the local. Each congregation speaks a universal

nomination active at this time. The Catholic church has a priest that comes from another town.)
Lakehills Church
Lakehills, Texas

We represent many church backgrounds—diverse denominations. Sharing crazy and zany moments represents to us "being fools for Christ." Faith seems to be our Friend. We see ourselves as free of cliques and openly accepting of all people. A variety of worship styles helps us grow.
Orchards Church
Vancouver, Washington

"In recent months, Jesus has taught me not to despise insignificant beginnings. Four years ago, two to seven persons met each Sunday. Some considered closing the congregation. Now, ten to seventeen join together each Sunday to talk, exchange verses from the Bible, and share concerns for prayers. We often pray together, not only during the service.

"When three children came, we started a children's class. For months, we had only three or four. Now there are more. But there had to be a start.

"When two mothers of young children met, because they were lonely, more mothers joined. Some had moved here after their marriages, and lost contact with their churches. In this way, a service for a certain group of persons was created.

"When two or three in the congregation want a Bible class, we begin.

"We read in Matthew 18:20: 'Where two or three are gathered in my name, there am I in the midst of them.'"
The United Methodist Church
Langenau, West Germany

*Here, O Lord, your servants gather,
hand we link with hand;
looking toward our Savior's cross,
joined in love we stand.
As we seek the realm of God,*

we unite to pray:
Jesus Savior, guide our steps,
for you are the Way.

Many are the tongues we speak,
scattered are the lands,
yet our hearts are one in God,
one in love's demands.
E'en in darkness hope appears,
calling age and youth:
Jesus, teacher, dwell with us,
for you are the Truth.

            Tokuo Yamaguchi, trans. Everett M. Stowe
            The United Methodist Hymnal, No. 552

Knox Memorial Church in the heart of Manila, The Philippines, has a membership of six thousand. The church holds six worship services in four languages every Sunday, and has sponsored five mission extensions which have become local churches in the last three years.

This actual, visible community, a company of men and women with ascertainable names and addresses, is the Church of God.

            Leslie Newbigin
            Household of God

When this area suffered a tornado and flood only ten days apart, this congregation responded automatically, turning our education building into a relief center. It was a place of lodging. It was the food and clothing distribution center. It was a people who hugged and cried with the victims. It was a people who spearheaded the Interfaith Group that remained active for one year to supply follow-up care to victims.

            First Church
            West Memphis, Arkansas

language of faith, but in the human language typical of that place. Each congregation gathers around symbols of Jesus Christ, but crosses, altars, elements of Communion, and decorations are made of local materials in the style of local people. Each congregation celebrates the mission of Jesus Christ to bring the whole world to salvation, but carries out that mission according to the needs of people in that region.

The tension of universal and local is a creative spring of vitality in the church. The congregation is a place where life in Christ is visible, where the community of faith is made actual. ***Everything is at stake in the life of the congregation.*** The congregation is a place where the faith must be made real. In the congregation, ways to concretely live out the claims of God's kingdom must be discovered. The congregation must point to the reign of God if we expect that reign to be anticipated anywhere.

When the faithful gather for worship in a given place, there is no "real" church someplace else of which this gathering is just a subdivision or a branch office. Christ is wholly present in each place; Christ is not divided. The responsibility for witness and service in Christ's name lies not somewhere else in some more pure and holy setting, but in each place where Christians gather. Christian response to world crises of war or environmental destruction lies not at some "higher level" of expertise or special knowledge, but in each congregation.

The church discovers its mission as particular assemblies of the faithful. Among ordinary people trying to balance multiple demands on their lives, the claims of God's intentions for the world must be spoken, defended, and acted on. At the same time, all our congregations are strengthened in mission by our covenant connection. Sharing our resources and supporting our common ministries, we are able to do far more together than we could ever do alone. ***Our congregations thrive when our connection reaches out in mission around the world. Our connection thrives when our congregations in each place are lively communities of faithful disciples.***

Community With Others

Another spring of vitality from the New Testament *ecclesia* is its nature as an open, public gathering. Paul violated every social norm with which he had been raised as a good Jew when he sought an audience for the gospel among the Gentiles. After a dream, blasphemous to a Jew, of a cosmic sheet containing all the creatures of God's good creation as sustenance for human life (Acts 10:9-16), Peter realized that the good news of Jesus Christ could not be confined to dietary laws or to the customs of one ethnic group.

The gospel was for everyone. Women had a central role in organizing and guiding the first congregations, in some cases offering their homes for meetings. The poor and the slaves of Mediterranean seaport cities heard the good news gladly. Christian discipleship did not always fit socially acceptable categories. It was a life available to people of every station and standing.

Congregations are open to all who hear the name of Christ and seek to follow him. In congregations the individual believer is confronted with other persons who hear things differently, who challenge her or his assumptions, who stretch her or his understanding of faith and its impact on daily living. Each person has a unique experience of Christ, and each person's life is changed and directed in a unique way. Yet there is only one Christ, and the people of congregations live and work together over time, united in his name.

Thus every congregation is a vivid example of the task of creating Christian community. Challenged by the model of communal sharing in the first congregation of Acts 2, sobered by the continual squabbles and food fights of the church at Corinth, each congregation must be built up in love by the Spirit to make best use of the gifts of the Spirit there. Each congregation must discover in its own way the full biblical promise of the blessings of hospitality to the stranger (Genesis 18:1-2; Hebrews 13:2).

The Christian congregation is the clearest continuing evidence of Christian faith across the centuries. From the very beginning, Christians have joined in fellowship with one another, for Christ promised his presence

"I am thankful for the diversity of people who belong to our church—although my 'head' tells me I would like to see more of a certain 'type' of people. I greatly appreciate the diversity which makes for a wider learning experience—more opportunity for individual growth as a child of God, in the Kingdom of God."

First Church
Olympia, Washington

An uneducated person may not feel comfortable in our congregation, because the structure of our service calls for a person to be able to read to fully participate. A street person may not feel comfortable because of the church's past reputation of "status" that has been a part of the community's consciousness.

Central Church
Atlanta, Georgia

The stained glass windows at Trinity Church in Sequim, Washington, lovingly crafted by a long-ago member, create beautiful and varying patterns of light in the sanctuary. The handmade pews and the meaningful message of the banners and paraments give the sanctuary the warmth and special ambiance of a place in which hundreds, long gone, prayed and worshiped.

Our Bible story? The wedding feast—joyful, loving, gathering together, serving, Jesus in the midst, miracles, humility, prayers answered.

Pioneer Church
Walla Walla, Washington

The theological task does not start anew in each age or each person. Christianity does not leap from New Testament times to the present as though nothing were to be learned from that great cloud of witnesses in between. For centuries Christians have sought to interpret the truth of the gospel for their time.

"Our Theological Task,"
The Book of Discipline, 1988, ¶69

Lord, make me an instrument of thy peace; where there is hatred, let me sow love; where there is injury, pardon;

whenever they gathered together. Christian discipleship cannot thrive apart from the community of fellow disciples. Through congregations of the faithful, people are formed in Christian obedience, hearing the biblical stories and being steeped in the images of faith: journey, wilderness, water, wine, bread, and harvest. Here the people are united with the communion of saints of all the ages who have left a rich legacy of prayer, witness and service.

Congregations are made up of people who seek the long turning around of their lives to face the horizon of abundant life in God's new creation. Without one another for support and inspiration, the people wither and their witness dies.

At the same time, like the *ecclesia* from which the church takes its name, congregations pray for and act on behalf of the common good of the wider community and society in which they have been given to minister. The witness of disciples belongs, after all, not primarily in the sanctuary, but in the everyday world for which God has given us responsibility as faithful stewards.

Living by the Stream of Wesleyan Heritage

I am the true vine, and my Father is the vinegrower. He removes every branch in me that bears no fruit. Every branch that bears fruit he prunes to make it bear more fruit. You have already been cleansed by the word that I have spoken to you. Abide in me, as I abide in you. Just as the branch cannot bear fruit by itself unless it abides in the vine, neither can you unless you abide in me. I am the vine, you are the branches. Those who abide in me and I in them bear much fruit, because apart from me you can do nothing. (John 15:1-5)

[This is the passage John Wesley chose for reading in the Wesleyan service of covenant renewal.]

United Methodism today draws life from the wellsprings of Christian faith through the ages. In saying the Apostles' Creed together, we who gather in United

Methodist congregations are united with Christians of every generation of the church; for the phrases of the creed have been recited by faithful Christians from the earliest days. In practicing the sacraments of baptism and Holy Communion, our congregations carry forward two essential acts of the church that have defined the church's life from the beginning, even though words, gestures, and interpretations have varied.

We often turn to the spiritual mothers and fathers of Christendom through the ages: Augustine of Hippo, Julian of Norwich, Thomas à Kempis, Teresa of Avila, Francis of Assisi, and many others. In psalms, hymns, and prayers recited by Christian congregations in every generation, United Methodists join a chorus of praise and supplication that began long before the Wesleys' lifetime.

Yet the Wesleyan movement brought to the flow of Christian history certain distinctive qualities that have characterized the Methodist family around the world for over 250 years. The freshness, energy, and intensity of John and Charles Wesley, and of the earliest Methodist preachers and their kindred spirits among Evangelicals and United Brethren, have been a deep source of life for the generations that have followed.

John Wesley was a priest in the Church of England and a teacher at Oxford. His youthful struggle for purity of faith and assurance of salvation matured into a rich and varied life as preacher, journalist, counselor, and pamphleteer. He was tireless in travel, unflagging in his zeal for preaching, and prolific in his correspondence. He touched the lives of countless people in Great Britain and other lands.

The central passion of Wesley's life was that people would know themselves to be saved, and would live a holy life in accord with the gospel. He had a genius for organization, and personally supervised, reprimanded, encouraged, and inspired the leaders who worked under him. But his thorough system of management was completely in the service of helping people know and live out their salvation in Christ.

Wesley did not call people out of the established Church of England. On the contrary, he required that

where there is doubt, faith;
where there is despair, hope;
where there is darkness, light;
and where there is sadness, joy.

O Divine Master,
grant that I may not so much seek
to be consoled as to console;
to be understood, as to understand;
to be loved, as to love;
for it is in giving that we receive,
it is in pardoning that we are pardoned,
and it is in dying that we are born to eternal life.
Francis of Assisi
The United Methodist Hymnal, No. 481

In the latter end of the year 1739 eight or ten persons came to Mr. Wesley, in London, who appeared to be deeply convinced of sin, and earnestly groaning for redemption. They desired, as did two or three more the next day, that he would spend some time with them in prayer, and advise them how to flee from the wrath to come, which they saw continually hanging over their heads. That he might have more time for this great work, he appointed a day when they might all come together, which from thenceforward they did every week, namely, on Thursday in the evening. To these, and as many more as desired to join with them (for their number increased daily), he gave those advices from time to time which he judged most needful for them, and they always concluded their meeting with prayer suited to their several necessities.

This was the rise of the United Society, first in Europe, and then in America. Such a society is no other than "a company of men having the form and seeking the power of godliness, united in order to pray together, to receive the word of exhortation, and to watch over one another in love, that they may help each other to work out their salvation."
The General Rules,
The Book of Discipline, 1988, ¶68

VITAL CONGREGATIONS—FAITHFUL DISCIPLES

Many members of the congregation are informed about the life and works of John Wesley and can quote from his writings. Many members have a family heritage in Methodism and can recall stories of camp meetings and circuit riders. Our church maintains a library which is rich in Methodist history and literature.

First Church
Bluefield, Virginia

*Depth of mercy! Can there be
mercy still reserved for me?
Can my God his wrath forbear,
me, the chief of sinners, spare?*

Charles Wesley
The United Methodist Hymnal, No. 355

The church must expect to be involved, and intimately so, with the divine, worldly, eschatological, historical regeneration. Indeed, we are involved, to the extent that we are Christ's church at all. If proof of this is needed, our Sunday morning congregations provide it week by week. We have the full range: from the casual enquirer, to the earnest seeker, to the habitual hanger-on, to the seasoned resister, to the faithful worker, to the unassuming saint. And the good news of the gospel, the gospel of light and salt and leaven and seed, is that in and through Jesus Christ, crucified, risen, and soon to come again, this very mixed community called church is as justified by grace as every one of us; as also is the world.

David Lowes Watson
General Board of Discipleship

Methodists attend public worship in their parish church and there receive the sacraments. He himself preached wherever people would hear him: in fields, town squares, meeting halls, sometimes even church buildings. But his purpose was not to alienate people from the church. He burned with a passion that they should know the salvation that awaits those who in repentance turn to the Lord, and that they be maintained in Christian living through the services of the church and the meetings of Methodist societies.

The Methodists' purpose of spiritual seriousness and holy living left an abiding stamp on both church and nation. Methodists never numbered more than a fraction of one percent of England's population during Wesley's lifetime; but their devotion and commitment was the talk of the land.

Many thousands heard the preaching of Wesley and others commissioned by him. Some of them also responded to his invitation to join a local Methodist society. These were open to all who had "a desire to flee from the wrath to come, to be saved from their sins." But upon entering the society, persons were immediately required to live by its rules. They were to show by their fruits in word and action their desire to be saved.

The societies were divided into class meetings, small groups in which the participants read Scripture and prayed together. They heard one another's struggles of faith and let their lives be examined in the bright light of gospel principles. Those in good standing were issued tickets granting them admission to the meetings. In their sins or backsliding they were reproved and sometimes even expelled.

The form and practice of class meetings became a distinctive mark of Methodism. Class meetings are still the basic unit of Methodist congregations in Nigeria and Korea, in the African Methodist Episcopal Church and many others. Class meetings are being encouraged in a variety of ways in United Methodism after a long period of neglect.

In eighteenth and nineteenth century North America the societies of Methodists became also congregations of the church. Congregations are open to people of all degrees of seriousness and seeking, not just those willing to undertake disciplines of holiness. Congregations of the church maintain the sacraments, requiring an ordained minister, and build up an order in continuity with the church through the ages. The circumstances of a new nation forced the Methodist societies to take on not only their inherited task of leading people to holiness, but also the broader churchly task of carrying forward the Christian tradition through Word, Sacrament, and Order.

Thus while Wesley did not originally intend for Methodist meetings to do anything but supplement and intensify the work of the Church of England, he and the leaders he designated for North America had to meet a changing situation by forming a separate church. They brought to the new organization all the genius of Wesley's system. They met in conferences annually to review their work and assign preachers to their posts. They elected general superintendents, soon called bishops, to travel throughout the land exhorting the people to hold fast to the ways of faith.

Above all the Methodists carried forward the unity once embodied in John Wesley's person, the sense that all Methodists are responsible for one another, sharing one another's burdens and joys, combining resources to accomplish the work of the church. Methodist congregations were not isolated, but connected with one another, bound in a covenant with one another and with God.

The mission undertaken by the first Methodist societies, "to reform the nation, particularly the church, and to spread scriptural holiness over the land," remains a vital task for United Methodism today. The twist is that United Methodism is now also "the church" in question, and we United Methodist people now face the question of whether and how to reform ourselves. To do so we will need to be fed by the springs of the Wesleyan heritage of faith.

A Serious Seeking

Methodism sought to touch the deepest levels of human life with the grace and love of God. Wesleyan

*Jesus, united by thy grace
and each to each endeared,
with confidence we seek thy face
and know our prayer is heard.*

Charles Wesley
The United Methodist Hymnal, No. 561

What may we reasonably believe to be God's design in raising up the preachers called Methodist?
Not to form any new sect; but to reform the nation, particularly the Church; and to spread scriptural holiness over the land.

John Wesley

*How can we sinners know
our sins on earth forgiven?
How can my gracious Savior show
my name inscribed in heaven?*

VITAL CONGREGATIONS—FAITHFUL DISCIPLES

*We who in Christ believe
that he for us hath died,
we all his unknown peace receive
and feel his blood applied.*

Charles Wesley
The United Methodist Hymnal, No. 372

The message of these early [Wesleyan] preachers was Jesus Christ: God's grace free in all, free to all, free for all. They preached Jesus who comes before we ask (prevenient grace), who pardons (justifying grace) and who cleanses and creates new life (sanctifying grace). Grace was their theme. Redemption of life was their hope.

Grace Upon Grace: The Mission Statement
of The United Methodist Church

We visit Rikers Island prison monthly for preaching, prayer, and moral support. On special occasions, such as Christmas, Thanksgiving, Mother's Day, we give them presents (personal need items). We give them Bibles and other religious literature. At Christmas, we celebrated with the inmates' children and gave them presents, had lunch together and shared in fellowship. Before this, we had visited them at home and we took presents to the homes of those who could not come to the Christmas program.

Iglesia Evangelica de Co-op City
Bronx, New York

John Wesley believed and taught an explicit doctrine of "holiness" as the goal and crown of the Christian life. "Sanctification," "perfect love," "Christian perfection" were various synonyms, in his vocabulary, for "holiness," and he rang the changes on this theme throughout his whole evangelistic career.

teaching responded to people's ultimate questions of the meaning and purpose of life, by pointing them to the glory of God and showing them the joy of Christian living.

For Methodists, Christian faith was a matter of life and death. It was a matter of a serious, fruitful life and a meaningful death. Many of the people touched by Methodist preaching labored under grueling conditions. Many were unable to find steady employment, or to work their way out of a spiral of debt that might drag them into prison. Death sat regularly at every family dinner table and visited every nursery. The struggle to grasp life's meaning under such social conditions was real and immediate.

From the Methodists, people heard that new life in Christ was available to all who earnestly sought it. No matter what one's past life had been, in Christ one could have a new birth: "that great change which God works in the soul when he brings it to life; when he raises it from the death of sin to the life of righteousness." Those whom God saved in Christ would be assured of seeing the face of God in glory, and thus need have no abiding fear of death.

Holy Living

But how could one's earnest desire of salvation, or one's new birth in Christ, be known except by the fruits of grace in holy living? Wesley made "scriptural holiness" the theme and melody to which all other Methodist teaching was but harmony and descant. Why should we be born again unless first for holiness, Wesley argued: "not a bare external religion, a round of outward duties [but] the image of God stamped upon the heart . . . the whole mind which was in Christ Jesus." And anyone who is in Christ would surely live accordingly, exhibiting his or her response to the prevening grace of God, the grace that "goes before" the believer stirring one to faith and assurance of salvation.

The societies laid out rules for such holy living. Participants were to show "their desire for salvation" by avoiding such evils as smuggling, usury, drunkenness, uncharitable conversation, wearing gold or costly apparel, and singing songs unsuited to the knowledge of God. Positively, they were to do good to others by "giving food to the hungry, by clothing the naked, by visiting or helping them that are sick, or in prison," and by supporting one another in necessities of life. And they were to join in the worship and sacraments of the church, to study Scripture and pray, while fasting regularly for their purity of soul, the money saved being given to the poor.

John Wesley elaborated on these rules whenever he thought Methodist people to be too casual in their manner. He despaired of what happened to Methodists when they began to acquire things. Do you not now think of yourself as "better than your poor, dirty neighbors? . . . How often do you fast? Is this not a duty to you, as much as to a day-laborer? . . . Are you not far less reprovable, far less advisable, than when you were poor?"

At the throne of judgment, Wesley cried, the Lord will inquire, "Didst thou employ that comprehensive talent, money . . . first supplying thy own reasonable wants, together with those of thy family; then restoring the remainder to me [the Lord] through the poor, whom I had appointed to receive it; looking upon thyself as only one of that number of poor?" Such works of mercy defined the Christian life; they were not optional. There was no holiness but social holiness.

Holiness was an all-embracing way of life that reflected the image of God in a person's heart. It was the fruit of being on the way to salvation, the outgrowth of God's grace acting in one's life. It was conversion in the sense of that lifelong turning toward perfection in love marked by complete faithfulness to Christ.

Wesley prescribed no one experience of conversion and salvation. He himself had felt his heart "strangely warmed" with the assurance that Christ's atonement was for him. But he did not require others to have a warm heart or any other single type of experience. What he did expect was that they desire salvation and live as though they meant it.

But Wesley was also sure that if holiness were reduced

All our truly human aspirations are self-transcending: they point to the love of God and neighbor as their true norms. But this is the essence of holiness. Inward holiness is, preeminently, our love of God, the love of God above all else and all else in God. Outward holiness is our consequent love of neighbor (all God's children, every accessible human being whom we may serve) with a love that springs from our love of God and that seeks the neighbor's well-being as the precondition of our own proper self-love.

Albert Outler
Theology in the Wesleyan Spirit

*I want a principle within
of watchful, godly fear,
a sensibility of sin,
a pain to feel it near,
I want the first approach to feel
of pride or wrong desire,
to catch the wandering of my will,
and quench the kindling fire.*

*Almighty God of truth and love,
to me thy power impart;
the mountain from my soul remove,
the hardness from my heart.
O may the least omission pain
my reawakened soul,
and drive me to that blood again,
which makes the wounded whole.*

Charles Wesley
The United Methodist Hymnal, No. 410

The Wesleyan emphasis on personal holiness can be a powerful source of fidelity in peacemaking. We affirm peacemaking as a sacred calling of the gospel, especially blessed by God, making us evangelists of shalom—peace that is overflowing with justice, compassion, and well-being. This holiness of peacemak-

ing as a vocation and lifestyle requires the constant nurture of our spiritual, moral, and physical strength.

Peacemaking is ultimately a spiritual issue. Without conversion of minds and hearts, the political systems of this world will remain estranged from shalom. The peaceable spirit can face the reality of the nuclear crisis with neither denial nor despair.

The Council of Bishops
Foundation Document,
In Defense of Creation

The United Methodist Church is tolerant and accepts other people's views. Our people look at the world view and not just ourselves.

Randolph Memorial Church
Kansas City, Missouri

Christian unity is founded on the theological understanding that in our Baptism, we are made members-in-common of the one Body of Christ. Christian unity is not an option; it is a gift to be received and expressed.

United Methodists respond to the theological, biblical, and practical mandates for Christian unity by firmly committing ourselves to the cause of Christian unity at local, national, and world levels. We invest ourselves in many ways by which mutual recognition of churches, of members, and of ministries may lead us to sharing in Holy Communion with all of God's people.

"Our Theological Task"
The Book of Discipline, 1988, ¶69

*Jesus, Lord, we look to thee,
let us in thy name agree;
show thyself the Prince of Peace,
bid our strife forever cease.*

to rules only, then Methodism would become a "dead sect," having the form but not the spirit of faithfulness. He urged the people to keep the rules "not for wrath but for conscience's sake," not just to go through the motions but because the Spirit was moving them to life with Christ.

Bound together "in society," Methodist people could build one another up in the faith, even while speaking the truth in love and reproving one another's shortcomings. Plain and direct in conversation, avoiding all gossip and slander, they could let the love of Christ be seen in their relationships with others.

Above all, the holy living of Methodists was to demonstrate the great commandment: love of God and love of neighbor. On the one hand, it required separation from a world dominated by pride, envy, greed and violence. On the other, it demanded even greater love for that world, so that everyone could have the opportunity to see and hear about the love and grace of God.

The Unity of Christians

John Wesley thrived on controversy and continually disputed the nature of salvation and the church with Calvinists, Roman Catholics, Anglicans, and all other comers. He was tireless in defending the Methodists against those who charged them with "enthusiasm," an empty-headed fervency of religious experience.

But for Wesley these were only family quarrels. Above all else he placed unity of spirit in the Christian community as the foremost expression of divine love. What is the church? he asked in one sermon. "A more ambiguous word than this is scarce to be found in the English language." Yet the catholic or universal church, he argued, by the Word of God is "all the persons in the universe whom God hath so called out of the world . . . as to be 'one body,' united by 'one Spirit,' having 'one faith, one hope, one baptism; one God and Father of all, who is above all, and through all, and in them all' " (Ephesians 4:4-6).

While holding to this universal truth, Wesley also referred to the definition in the Articles of Religion of the Church of England (*The Book of Discipline, 1988*, ¶68). There the church is described as "a congregation of faithful men"; and this concrete sense of church as, in his own words, "a congregation, or body of people, united together in the service of God," was foundational for him.

In his sermon on the "Catholic [Universal] Spirit" that is the essence of Christian unity, he argued that "a catholic spirit is not indifference to all congregations." A spirit of unity with other Christians does not mean that it should not really matter which congregation one joins. On the contrary, a person of "truly catholic spirit . . . is fixed in his congregation as well as his principles. . . . There he partakes of all the ordinances of God. There he receives the supper of the Lord. . . . There he rejoices to hear the word of reconciliation, the gospel of the grace of God . . . These his nearest, his best-loved brethren . . . he watches over in love, as they do over his soul. . . . These he regards as his own household."

In other words, there are no disciples in general. There are only those who participate in actual congregations, where their love of God and neighbor is nourished.

Yet while Christians are gathered into congregations, indeed "united by the tenderest and closest ties to one particular congregation," their hearts are also "enlarged toward all mankind," embracing everyone far and near in universal love. All congregations are thus bound together by their common faith in a God who is love. All who proclaim Jesus Christ as Lord, who love God and neighbor, who abstain from evil and are "zealous of good works," enjoy the unity of the Spirit in the bond of peace.

Thus Wesley described the balance of universal and local that should be present in congregational life. Each congregation is unique, with its own peculiar mix of participants and local practices. Yet each shares a common spirit of love and holiness.

The Methodists made this common spirit concrete through the minutes or records of their annual conferences, and later through *The Book of Discipline*

*By thy reconciling love
every stumbling block remove;
each to each unite, endear;
come, and spread thy banner here.*

Charles Wesley
The United Methodist Hymnal, No. 562

Theologically, we demonstrate a hunger for the gifts of the Holy Spirit. We embrace the Wesleyan traditions. We have used different methods of baptism. We embrace people coming into membership. We also invite all who want to participate in holy communion—a distinctive United Methodist trait. We feel that most of us are traditional Wesleyans, more or less.

The Community Church
Morgantown, West Virginia

A 70-year-old industrialist and owner of a tennis hall became acquainted with a sportsman who belongs to our church, and he joined the congregation.

A girl became friends with a member of our church and decided to join the Bible class.

Vital congregations can be found where the refreshing life of God is not confined in pious hearts or enclosed in church buildings, but where it is brought out to places where Jesus Christ is unknown or rejected.

Vital congregations occur where Christians cease to meet in their "club houses" in order to exchange pious vocabulary as philatelists exchange their stamps.

The United Methodist Church
Wangen, West Germany

VITAL CONGREGATIONS—FAITHFUL DISCIPLES

Ever since John Wesley began to refer to the scattered Methodist classes, bands and societies throughout eighteenth-century England as "the connexion," Methodists everywhere have embraced the idea that as a people of faith we journey together in connection and in covenant with one another.
　　　　　　　　　　The Book of Discipline, 1988, ¶112

*O Breath of Life, come sweeping through us,
revive your church with life and power.
O Breath of Life, come, cleanse, renew us,
and fit your church to meet this hour.*

*O Breath of Love, come, breathe within us,
renewing thought and will and heart.
Come, love of Christ, afresh to win us;
revive your church in every part.*
　　　　　　　　　　Bessie Porter Head
　　　　The United Methodist Hymnal, No. 543

containing the doctrines and rules of all Methodists. That it is called a "book of discipline" and not a "book of order" or laws, speaks volumes about the character of Methodism. The Wesleys started a way of life, a pattern of holy living. The discipline for this life provides a framework through which congregations of disciples can remain faithful to the task. What unites the United Methodists is our common discipline of holiness and our shared movement for reforming the church and the continents.

This is the real meaning of the "connection" in which we are covenant partners. Not so much our institutional ties or our financial support, as our mutual commitment and constant prayers for one another, constitute the connection. United in love, we United Methodists hope to be a worthy reflection of the infinite love of God made known in Jesus Christ.

Living As Congregations by Memory and Hope

Let the word of Christ dwell in you richly; teach and admonish one another in all wisdom, and with gratitude in your hearts sing psalms, hymns, and spiritual songs to God. (Colossians 3:16)

The good news of Jesus Christ has found a home with countless people across the centuries. The witness of the Holy Spirit through the church has found a home in countless congregations of Christians who gather for worship and service.

There is but "one Lord, one faith, one baptism," one story of salvation to which we all strive to be faithful (Ephesians 4:5). Our unity as Christians and as United Methodists of every land and culture is a gift of God to be celebrated and treasured.

Yet our unity is precious to us, ironically, because we are not all alike. We enjoy unity, but not uniformity. We are of both sexes, and of many colors, many ethnic heritages, many nationalities. We are located in many different contexts of ministry, rural and urban, poor and prosperous. One of the Spirit's most profound gifts is that the gospel story is infinitely adaptable, allowing each believer and each congregation to find a home within it in a way suited to the upbuilding of Christian faith and life.

By water and the Spirit each congregation is given a distinctive call and special gifts to be acted upon in a unique way in a particular place. Each congregation has its own identity. Each congregation is a rich fabric of the stories of persons, events, and relationships interwoven through the joys and trials of life together. Each congregation assembles in a certain place and relates to its neighborhood in its own way.

Too often as a denomination we do not treat congregations as unique. We develop regional or national programs and goals, and hope they will trickle down to be "applied" in congregations. We emphasize congregational performance on institutional scales of membership and money. Our appointive system has sometimes encouraged pastors to think that all congregations are basically alike and can be ministered with in more or less the same way. But to overlook the realities of congregational variety is to miss the wealth of resources that are available to the church's mission.

Especially for those among us who are white North Americans, it has been difficult to see our congregations as unique. We have thought of our way of worshiping, making decisions, and organizing for mission, as normative—simply the way things are done in the church. We have not seen how our ways of talking and behaving with one another express our own unique culture. And because white North American experience has been considered the norm, we have had little reason to be aware of our history. Those among us who comprise ethnic groups that are in the minority in North America, have taught and celebrated our own history far more, and have had a stronger sense of the special mission of our congregations in our communities.

Amazing things begin to happen when the people of a congregation break through their world of assumptions. When they stop seeing themselves as the norm, and their way of doing things as just "the way things are," they get a whole new perspective on their local church's task.

As a church, we feel a special closeness in working together. At a time when the church needed firewood for heating, we joined in work to prepare that wood. Then, when the church no longer needed to be heated in that manner, we started an annual Groundhog Supper. The men of the church prepare and serve a meal. They grind and stuff sausage, grind wheat and prepare pancakes, and churn ice cream.

Lyona Church
Junction City, Kansas

The church originally built on this spot in 1840 was replaced by the current structure in 1917. The old church had bed bugs, and the lumber from it was used to build a barn which eventually had to be torn down and burned. The stained-glass sign over the entrance says "M. E. Church, South," and is being removed and mounted for historical purposes as a new one with Cross and Flame is being constructed and installed. This was the church in 1865 where the "Palmyra Manifesto" was framed and submitted to the Southern Church which, when it was accepted, kept that church separate from the M. E. Church immediately after the Civil War.

The United Methodist Church
Palmyra, Missouri

In 1973, a group of high school and college students, some missionaries, and some lay people were encouraged by the late Bishop S. Trowen Nagbe to organize a Sunday School and an evening service for those young people who could not afford to ride to downtown Monrovia to the First United Methodist Church.

Two years later, the enrollment in the Sunday School and the membership in the evening service had grown beyond expectation. A congregation was organized in memory of Bishop Nagbe in 1975. Today the S. Trowen Nagbe Church in Sinkor, Monrovia, Liberia, has a membership of over seven hundred.

VITAL CONGREGATIONS—FAITHFUL DISCIPLES

Give thanks for the past, for those who had vision,
who planted and watered so dreams could come true.
Give thanks for the now, for study, for worship,
for mission that bids us turn prayer into deed.

Give thanks for tomorrow, full of surprises,
for knowing whatever tomorrow may bring,
the Word is our promise always, forever,
we rest in God's keeping and live in God's love.

Jane Marshall
The United Methodist Hymnal, No. 87

Hope Publishing Co.; 380 S. Main Pl.; Carol Stream, IL 60188.

First Church helped establish Beckley College. The first classes were held in the church. One of the students threw his pen up to the rafters in the sanctuary and it is still fastened there after all these years!

First Church
Beckley, West Virginia

The pews were purchased from an abandoned church in lower Michigan for about $100 for the entire lot, and then they were trucked to our church. Ironically, the Michigan church re-opened later and had to purchase new pews. The pews are unique—each is slanted back and the entire pew is curved into an arc shape. This is said to be for large families so mom and dad can sit in the center and keep an eye on their brood in either direction without having to lean forward!

East Springfield Church
LaGrange, Indiana

"At our first charge conference we were voting on the budget and it was a very serious meeting. My daughter was only two years old and voted a resounding 'NO' to the proposed budget plan (which passed nonetheless)."

Flame of Faith Church
West Fargo, North Dakota

They are led to a deeper and wiser cherishing of their past. They see more clearly the features that make them distinctive. They are better able to name the gifts and strengths given them by the Holy Spirit.

Congregations that are in touch with their own identity and community context are much better able to define their purpose and involve their people in concrete acts of discipleship. They receive a fresh imagination about the ministry and mission that is open to them in the place they have been given to serve.

Story

The story of the salvation that God offers us in Jesus Christ is the heart and soul of our life together in the church. **Our task is to find our place in the story so that God can write the next chapters through us.** And in order to find our place we need to examine our story as people of God to see how it reflects and continues the gospel story.

Every congregation has a story to tell. In part it is composed of the life stories of its participants over the years. In the main, it is a story of the corporate life of the faith community in that place. The congregation's story is also part of larger stories of the society in which it is located and the world events that have influenced them. And each congregation's story reveals the struggle of disciples to be faithful to the story of God's outreaching love for us made known in Jesus Christ.

People love to tell stories. Ask a person why she is a member of a particular local church, and she will most likely tell you the story of how she came to be active there. Ask someone what it means to be a Christian, and he will probably tell you a story of his journey in faith.

Congregations are alive with stories. New members do not usually feel fully part of things until they begin to learn these stories. Behind everything a local church does, behind every object in its building, behind every participant, there is a story. In the repeating of them these stories help give a congregation its unique identity.

Sometimes anecdotes about things that happened years ago are waved off as nostalgia for the good old days. Other stories are put down as mere gossip. On the contrary, stories are what make a congregation what it is, and they both teach and remind participants of their identity.

Every congregation needs to tell its story. This is especially constructive when a new pastor arrives, or when planning for mission is underway. The gifts and strengths that make the congregation uniquely what it is are much easier to name when examining the story. Here is a local church, for example, that has lived and struggled with the successes and sufferings of its rural farming constituency. Or here is another that has had a major impact on the adjacent university campus through the participation of professors, staff, and students. Or here is yet another that chose to stay downtown in the city and develop a ministry with new people, often poor and uprooted from their family homes, moving into the neighborhood.

Here is a local church with a long-standing interest in the arts, which has attracted many people who express their faith through painting, weaving, pottery, and sculpture. Or here is another that has a lot of new Christians and people seeking to know more about Jesus Christ, a congregation that values openness and encouragement of questions about the faith. Or here is yet another that has a strong sense of friendship and mutual caring, in which the participants are bound together with cords of love expressed whenever people are sick or unemployed or in any kind of grief and suffering.

Whatever gifts and strengths are clear from the story can be claimed as part of God's mission in the world. Jesus taught by parables, simple stories using images from everyday life. A congregation's story is also a parable with an image (or images) that reveals a deeper truth. The themes of Scripture can be seen woven through the congregation's journey together.

One congregation comes to see itself as an Exodus church: one that finds itself in unfamiliar surroundings, through the changes of town or city. Now it is experiencing the wilderness of a lack of resources or uncertain direction. It is learning to wait upon the Lord to provide the gifts it needs for the continuing journey.

Or another sees itself as a resurrection church: one

History records that United Brethren services were first conducted in Fairview Township in a stone school building located in what is now known as New Market. A young and ardent pastor, Reverend John Fohl, stationed at Shopps Station of the United Brethren Church, Shiremanstown, Pennsylvania, is believed to have started these meetings. In 1842, Reverend Fohl was invited to preach at Prowell's School House.

On April 22, 1844, at a Quarterly Conference held in Fishing Creek Valley, John S. Prowell, Henry B. Kauffman and Jacob G. Miller were appointed as the first trustees of the congregation's property. The church building was begun, finished, and dedicated in 1844. Thus Salem (frequently referred to in early days as the "Stone" Church) became the first church building constructed by any denomination in Fishing Creek Valley. The native brown sandstone used in the walls of the building was obtained from the nearby farm of Jacob H. Haldeman. Much of the work was done by members and friends of the congregation.

The building had two front entrances—one for women and one for men. There was an aisle leading to the pulpit from each of the two doorways, with a row of seats on either side of each aisle. A divider ran through the center of the church to separate men from women. It was considered improper for men and women to be seated together in church. Each side had a stove for heat.

The value of the building was about $1,000. For approximately thirty years, the support for the ministerial service was $40.00 annually.

Fishing Creek Salem Church
Etters, Pennsylvania

The stained glass window of Jesus is particularly meaningful to members of Covenant Church in Dothan, Alabama. One member sees Jesus' eyes following him wherever he goes in the sanctuary. Another comments how the racial look of Christ changes as the light changes. One sees Jesus holding his hands "out for me," and another sees the window as symbolic of the church—"Covenant's arms are out for everyone."

As in the biblical communities, memory and vision and identity and mission are necessary and interrelated in the life of modern congregations. Those who stress memory and identity exclusively (e.g., Bible reading as a devotional end in itself apart from mission) run the risk of becoming the fossil church. A fossil is an extraordinarily faithful witness to the past, but it is incapable of responding to the present or the future. Those who stress vision and mission without maintaining a rootedness in faith memory run the risk of becoming the chameleon church. Having no identity of its own, it is likely to take on the coloration of whatever ideology, cultural context, or fad happens to surround it.

Both memory and vision are necessary to an adequate theology of the church for every congregation. Rootedness in our past tradition and trust in God's future is what frees us from the tyranny of the present.

Bruce C. Birch
"Memory in Congregational Life"
in Congregations: Their Power to Form and Transform

We see ourselves after the order of Barnabas, especially in his defense of Paul who sought admission to the church after his conversion. The members of the church were afraid of Paul because he had been cruelly persecuting the Christians. Barnabas that virtually died out at one point, but through an infusion of new people has found new life and mission in its neighborhood. Yet another is a "treasure hidden in a field" church (Matthew 13:44): one that has taken a risk of establishing a new ministry in a community, in the faith that there is a treasure of new Christians with their gifts for discipleship to be found there.

By telling their story, and seeking to understand it more fully, congregations are led to a richer sense of God's working in their lives. Like those who listened to Jesus' parables, their eyes are opened to new avenues of ministry and mission in Christ's name that build on their strengths and draw them toward further growth in Christian discipleship. They are challenged to think about what they want a future generation to tell about them, or how their children will someday view their faithfulness. Their story is essential to their vitality, and in telling it they receive new imagination for their mission.

Symbol

Just as the gospel story is captured in the symbol of the cross, so stories cluster around the symbols that grace our congregations. Every Christian congregation hallows, and is hallowed by, symbols of its faith and life together.

Often we are unconscious of all the meanings behind a symbol. Sometimes we are careless about our symbols and do not use them as we might to enrich the experience of believers. But through a sensitivity and awareness of symbols, congregations can help shape the lives of participants toward a more disciplined life with Christ.

A symbol can be any object that points beyond itself to some larger memory or meaning. The cross is universal, of course. Yet in every congregation even the cross looks a little different, or is placed differently. And people in that faith community come to associate particular meanings with it.

For example, in one congregation the cross is made of metal, carefully hammered and polished by craftsmen from a local church on the other side of the globe, and

HEARING THE WORD OF GOD

sent as a gesture of thanksgiving and friendship in Christ. When people look at the cross, they realize that Christ transcends all boundaries of nation and race.

In another congregation, the cross is finely carved wood, a work of love by a man paralyzed from the waist down but gifted with woodworking skills. Before he died, this was the only way he could really express his love for Christ and desire to follow him. And when the congregation looks there, they remember his faithfulness.

Likewise other objects are rich with memories. Here is a chair for the preacher to sit in, a gift of Dr. Hoffmann's family. He was a missionary in China and shared the hope of many that Christianity can be a redeeming force in that land. Here is a set of chimes on the wall, donated by an adult Sunday school class during the Depression of the 1930's as a sign of their determination that the church would not close because of financial problems. Or here are benches for worshipers to sit on, purchased with money from the sale of one family's property.

Congregations are strengthened by the memories and meanings attached to such symbols. By taking time to reflect on the objects around them, they can discover a deeper commitment to ministry. In passing on the meanings to the next generation, they will help give them a fuller sense of how to live with faithfulness.

Symbols are not monuments. When they become simply memorials to people or events no longer alive, symbols can deaden a congregation's life. The vitality of symbols comes from their expression of life with Christ. As they point people to a living Christ who calls disciples to follow into the challenges of today and tomorrow, they call out a new sense of oneness with those who have gone before.

Congregations are sometimes careless with their symbols. It is not unusual to see a baptismal font shoved into the corner collecting dust. This congregation apparently does not expect to be baptizing anyone into the faith anytime soon. They appear to have little awareness of their own baptism and thus of their own calling to carry forward the ministry of Christ. Many

came to his defense and persuaded the church to give him a chance. We believe we have some of those same qualities. However, as we consider seriously our sense of who might not feel comfortable in our church, it seems apparent that we are not communicating this sort of acceptance. This is something we are going to have to struggle with.

First Church
Lawndale, North Carolina

Lift high the cross, the love of Christ proclaim till all the world adore his sacred name.

George William Kitchin and
Michael Robert Newbolt
The United Methodist Hymnal, No. 159

Hope Publishing Co.; 380 S. Main Pl.; Carol Stream, IL 60188.

A statue by a local and renowned artist hangs above the main entrance to Hockessin Church. It has become a symbol of our church in the community. The statue is Joseph of Arimathea carrying the body of Christ in his outstretched arms.

The theme of sacrificial offering is maintained inside the church. The cross is lifted high and hangs suspended above the altar.

Hockessin Church
Hockessin, Delaware

The wooden cross means a lot to a number of people because it was made from the altar rail from the old sanctuary.

The United Methodist Church of Hastings
Hastings, Minnesota

VITAL CONGREGATIONS—FAITHFUL DISCIPLES

The pulpit is sacred and not to be used except through those who proclaim the message of God.

Wesley Chapel Church
Lincoln, Delaware

The sanctuary is a very new place. The former building that housed the sanctuary area was torn down because of inherent structural damage. There was a lot of pain and division over the tearing down of that building. But out of the ashes arose a Phoenix and things have been looking a whole lot better. We believe that in the past too much attachment was placed in the building and not on the people. It was a shrine more than a house of worship. The new building has brought about some new beginnings and new integrity.

First Church
Brady, Texas

Our church was rebuilt after a fire in 1942. The furniture came from a dissolved church and the contention about using it almost tore the church apart. Sometimes it is very hard to give up the old, but we have adjusted. We have an old pulpit that was saved from the fire because it was being used at the school for Baccalaureate. It holds a place of honor at the front of the sanctuary.

Vinland Church
Baldwin, Kansas

Our present sanctuary is only 26 years old. It brings back memories of the building of the church and the work that went into the merger of the three churches that came together to become the present Kent Island Church. Younger members are attached to this building, because they remember confirmation classes where they learned about spaces and objects in the building and why they are there.

Kent Island Church
Chester, Maryland

congregations use tasteless round wafers as the "bread" for Communion, thus denying themselves the rich associations fresh-baked bread has with the biblical words: "Because there is one bread, we who are many are one body, for we all partake of the one bread" (1 Corinthians 10:17).

Congregations need to do a careful job of educating new participants about the meaning of symbols. Newcomers do not feel welcome, for example, in a room full of portraits of past leaders about whom they know nothing. They feel awkward at the Communion rail if the method of distributing the bread and cup has not been explained. They may not understand why money is being spent to repair the lighted cross atop the steeple. If only they knew that many workers in the factory on the hill opposite the church building have said how much it comforts them to look out the window and see it glowing there on the night shift!

Many gestures and actions in a congregation also have symbolic meaning. Pastors lift their hands in benediction. Choirs process from outside to the front of the sanctuary. People stand to sing, especially when praising God. They often bow their heads to pray. Through such patterns, believers are shaped in the ways of faith. They learn the forms of reverence that will help them live with devotion each day.

Some gestures and actions are unintended, though, or convey unconscious meanings. About these, congregations need continually to ask, are they communicating something important about Christian faith? Does the fact that all the ushers taking up the offering in worship are men over fifty say something about who is considered worthy to handle the church's money? Does the way everyone walks single file out one door after services convey something about the sense of Christian community in that place?

What do the locked doors of the church building tell the community about the Christian witness there? What is communicated about the congregation's sense of hospitality when strangers visit the worship service and, especially if they are not dressed like everyone else or do not smell clean, are automatically referred to the pastor?

Symbols abound in a local church. Through careful attention to them, congregations can keep them alive with meaning, and can use them to help shape their life of discipleship.

Language

Stories are told in words that become precious to us. We sometimes disagree about translations of the Bible, or the wording of songs and prayers, because we really do care about the language in which we express our faith.

Language is a distinctive part of every congregation's identity. Just like families or schools or businesses, congregations learn to talk to one another in ways they will understand. A kind of jargon develops for the people's way of talking about their faith or about events in their lives.

Through songs, prayers, words of praise, sermons, even through announcements made in worship service, a congregation communicates who it believes God is, and what Jesus Christ means to them. People learn words and phrases that help them talk about their faith. "O come, all ye faithful"—"Almighty God, unto whom all hearts are open, all desires known"—"Shall we gather at the river"—"We would like to say a special word of welcome to our visitors this morning"—"This is the day that the Lord hath made"—"The doors of the church are open"—"Let us join our hearts and minds in prayer."

In these and myriad other words, congregations learn of God's grace and mercy; they hear the stories of Jesus; they develop attitudes of hope and expectation; they are led to sharper awareness of the needs of others. Through the language of faith, children learn what people in their congregation believe and trust to be true.

One of the disturbing patterns in many congregations is the absence of much language about Christian faith, apart from the "official" words used in worship. The last thing one would expect to hear at a fellowship dinner or coffee hour is anyone talking about God. In many local

---

There is a picture of Colonel Ives in the entryway. Sometime, way back, the church was in trouble for back taxes and he paid $35 to save it. He then "crowed" about how he had saved the church and had them change the name from whatever it was to "Ives Chapel."

Ives Chapel Church
Baldwin City, Kansas

In the United Methodist Church of Corrigan, Texas, one Sunday morning the pastor called for the ushers to come forward to receive the offering of the people. On this particular morning, no men stood up to take the offering. After a short time, a mentally retarded lady in her mid-twenties stood up and came forward to take the offering. The next Sunday she assumed the role herself and was joined by another retarded lady in the congregation. These two ladies are now the greeters and the ushers, taking up the morning offering in worship. God does move congregations to change.

We do not necessarily use terms like "atonement" and "salvation" in our everyday conversations, but we do talk about answered prayers and God's working in our lives.

First Church
Rutherfordton, North Carolina

We do not use "Bible language" or terms; our language is more often that of academe—from psychology, sociology, etc.

Wesley Church
Urbana, Illinois

VITAL CONGREGATIONS—FAITHFUL DISCIPLES

There is a strong emphasis on Bible study and a biblical basis for action within most groups in the church. We freely use such biblical terms as sin and deliverance, gifts, and covenants when facing life's challenges and golden moments—marriage, childbirth, baptism, confirmation, divorce, unemployment, illness, death.

Manchester Church
Manchester, Missouri

Although Bible language and terms are often used just for the sake of using them and, hence, lose their meaning, we should use them more than we do. Certain words and phrases have been snatched from us by our more fundamental or evangelical friends. We tend to avoid words such as "saved" or "salvation." Because of the connotation and association these words and terms have come to represent, we have "disowned" them and consider ourselves "too sophisticated" to use them. We perhaps should redefine these terms and words in a way that makes them meaningful for our congregation and community.

Trinity Church
Duncanville, Texas

First Church in Statesboro, Georgia, is a downtown church on Main Street, two blocks from the county court house. It is located in a city of about 23,000 with a college of about 10,500. Members come from throughout the city and county.

churches the pastor is the only person ever asked to pray at the beginning of a meeting or event. And people who are comfortable talking about the presence of Christ in their lives are often tagged as the "spiritual types."

Congregations need to ask themselves if they are adequately training people in the language of faith. Many people simply do not know and have never heard words of comfort or prophetic challenge, or words that would help them understand their own faith questions, or words they could use to tell others about their faith in Christ.

Language is a rich resource in congregational life. When it becomes a jargon that only insiders understand, it can exclude others. But when it is alive with images of our walk with God, it can lead people to fuller understanding of their life of discipleship.

Context

Each congregation's story is a unique weaving of personal and corporate stories, and of memories and meanings attached to symbols, told in a distinctive language. But each story is also unique because it has a particular setting or context.

Every congregation meets in a neighborhood. Every one has a setting to which it must relate. How the congregation views its neighborhood, and how the people in the community view the congregation, has everything to do with the effectiveness of the local church's mission.

Our heritage teaches us that God's grace is universal, that salvation in Christ is available to everyone who comes to God with a repentant heart. We sing this belief in our hymns. Our children understand it when they sing "Jesus Loves Me." People need to experience the love, acceptance, and openness that so often mark our congregations. The congregation that turns its back on its community misses the chance to tell others of the grace and love of God.

Congregations are made vital by a continuing awareness of the changes and needs in their neighborhoods. In the USA and many other countries, a census report is regularly available from government agencies. It shows not only how many people live in a neighborhood, but also how old they are, their marital status, numbers of children, income level, types of employment, and many other factors. Census reports offer an accurate picture of neighborhood trends, sometimes surprising ones, showing the presence of new groups—single parents, immigrants from another country, unemployed or destitute persons—to whom a congregation can reach out with new ministries.

But congregations also need to see neighborhood people face to face, and to find out how the church is perceived. In the USA especially most people come to the church building by automobile. They never really walk in the neighborhood or meet the people. Church members might well find, to their chagrin, that they are seen as outsiders, driving into the area and going inside their building, not really interested in what is going on around them. Residents begin to assume that "the church doesn't care."

People from the congregation need to talk to people on the street or to community leaders, asking them what is going on in the area, what changes are taking place, what the needs of the area are. If these persons have never heard of the church's work here, the members get a sharp idea of how they are perceived.

By walking in the area around the church building, members of a congregation can begin to see what their building looks like to strangers and how it would feel to approach it for the first time. Many church buildings are difficult to find unless one knows where to look. Many are hidden by hills, trees, or other buildings, depending on the setting.

Many have high walls and windows that no one can see through to know what might be going on inside. Doors are often shut tight and locked. Many buildings have few signs or other indication of which door to enter. Some do not even say on the outside what the building is. All of these factors tell strangers or newcomers that they may not really be welcome here.

Congregations with vitality in Christ communicate a

Toney Church in Toney, Alabama, is in a rural area that is becoming a bedroom for industry in Huntsville.

Ripley Church is a rural congregation in Dexter, Maine. The only business in town is the corner store. The children are bused to school in another town. There are a few small farms which are not highly productive.

Leslie Church in Leslie, Georgia, is located in an area that grows peanuts, cotton, soybeans, and corn. Lack of job opportunities is leading people to leave the community.

Interlachen is a rural town thirty miles east of the University of Florida. We are fast becoming a bedroom community for Jacksonville, Gainesville, Palatka, and Ocala. Rapid growth is accompanied by lots of loneliness for our residents.
First Church of Interlachen
Interlachen, Florida

Bowen's Creek Church in Roark, Kentucky, is along a rural creek. 78 people live on the creek; 44 are members of the church, and the rest are affiliated or constituency. Bowen's Creek is in the heart of Appalachia. Local employment is mostly coal. Forty-six percent of the people are employed in the coal industry, sixteen percent retired, thirty-three percent unemployed, and five percent employed elsewhere.

VITAL CONGREGATIONS—FAITHFUL DISCIPLES

The neighborhood is considered upper middle class. Yet, we are in the southern fringes of the San Gabriel Valley where there is an upsurge of gang activity, homelessness, and hunger.
First Filipino-American Church
Hacienda Heights, California

The people are not only spiritually poor but also economically poor. The community is plagued by various kinds of social ills including drugs, alcohol, dropouts, unemployment, broken homes, homeless people, racism and racial violence, all sorts of crimes and prostitution. The duty of the church is to address these social problems and concerns with effective evangelism and social programs.
Wesley Church
New Haven, Connecticut

The chair of the Long-Range Planning Committee at Wintersville Church in Wintersville, Ohio, is an 82-year-old who is concerned about where the church is going. He doesn't hide behind tradition but will step out and try something new. Thinking of his sense of humor, someone described him as "a corker."

Let's celebrate God's love. We have the opportunity to know God better and to better relate to each other through First United Methodist Church.

Let's celebrate our staff. They provide experiences which help us to be aware of this love and God's purpose for our lives.

Let's celebrate our beautiful world. God gives us the world to protect and preserve for those who follow us.

spirit of openness. They are active in their community, known for responding to needs. They work with other institutions such as schools, hospitals, housing projects, or businesses. They face their neighborhoods with open doors, and continually find ways to invite people to join in a journey of discipleship with Christ.

The Ministry and Mission of the Local Church

Our task as congregations is to find our place in the story of God's outreaching love, and to discover by God's grace how we can become a new chapter in the story of Christ's ministry. To meet these challenges requires self-awareness and intentional planning based firmly on our hope in Christ.

Planning, after all, is hope made concrete and visible. We make plans to serve the needs of our communities and our world because our hope is in One who served others in all things. We tell our own story, and name our gifts and strengths, so that we can plan how best to use our resources as a sign of God's reign.

Fed by springs of vitality from our heritage, our congregations are empowered by the Holy Spirit for the ministry and mission of tomorrow's church. We drink from deep wells. In the story of Jesus we know the assurance of salvation and hear the call to discipleship. Through the action of the Spirit, we receive new vision and determination to be congregations of lively witness and active service. In reviewing the character of the church from its beginnings, we are reminded of our purpose. In the voices of John and Charles Wesley we hear both grace and challenge. And in recalling our own stories, we are refreshed with a sense of our strengths for our mission in the places we are given to serve.

The United Methodist connection holds in covenant community this immense variety of congregations. Through our mutual support as congregations in covenant, we share resources and hold one another up in the joys and sorrows of ministry. Together we undergird the world outreach of the church and support ministries in every walk of life.

But the connection is only as vital as the congregations that comprise it. From congregations alive with a firm sense of identity and mission flow the streams that together make a river of witness. Our prayer is always that God will cause to well up in each congregation in each place a spring to water the tree of faith. So may we as faithful disciples bear fruit for the reign of God.

It is difficult to believe on a beautiful spring morning when dew sparkles on the grass, and birds sing in the trees, that our world, God's creation, is dying. But it's true, and it may already be too late to save it. We who inhabit the earth have altered the land, the air, and the water so much that the effects are being felt in every country on the planet. It is predicted, if this situation is not changed during the next decade, the earth will no longer be able to sustain life.

We understand that God created all people. We heard our pastor quote Matthew 25: "As you do it to the least of these [my people] you do it to me." Is our caring for the world and its people superficial?
How can I relate to the starving of the world when my supermarket is well-stocked?
How can I relate to the refugees and homeless when I have a comfortable bed?
Why should I concern myself with the 37 million people in the United States who can't afford health insurance? My policy is paid up.

Do we still believe in the "survival of the fittest" even though survival now depends upon cooperation between all interconnected life systems?
Do we still believe "rugged individualism" is the "American Way" when increasing numbers of people are being squeezed into poverty by the greed and corruption of Corporate America?
Do we still believe the business of the world doesn't belong in our churches? If we close the door on the creation, we close the door on the Creator.

Let's celebrate! Never before in the history of the world has God challenged us as God challenges us today.

First Church
Marshalltown, Iowa

CLAIMING OUR BAPTISM

Through the Word, God invites us to Christian discipleship. All who are captured by the vision God reveals to us are invited to serve the Lord. The doors of the church are open; all are welcome to join the fellowship of Christ.

The church is the covenant community of the baptized: those whom God has called by grace, and who have responded in faith. Through baptism we are cleansed by the water of God's forgiveness and blessed by the gifts of the Holy Spirit. We are initiated into the family of faith to assume our place in the Body. We are given our true vocation as witnesses to the hope that is within us.

In remembering our baptism we affirm the claim God has upon us, and renew our covenant pledge to be faithful disciples. Putting our lives at God's disposal, we commit ourselves to ministry in Christ's name. Through the congregation of the faithful to which we belong, we are prepared, encouraged, and commissioned for our ministry in the world.

VITAL CONGREGATIONS—FAITHFUL DISCIPLES

The Holy Spirit work within you, that being born through water and the Spirit, you may be a faithful disciple of Jesus Christ.

Baptismal Covenant I
The United Methodist Hymnal, page 37

St. Paul Church in Clarksdale, Mississippi, was established thirty years ago and is beginning to confirm its third generation as members. Baptism is especially meaningful as this congregation continues to grow.

In those days Jesus came from Nazareth of Galilee and was baptized by John in the Jordan. And just as he was coming up out of the water, he saw the heavens torn apart and the Spirit descending like a dove on him. And a voice came from heaven, "You are my Son, the Beloved; with you I am well pleased."

Mark 1:9-11

*Wash, O God, our sons and daughters,
where your cleansing waters flow.
Number them among your people;
bless as Christ blessed long ago.
Weave them garments bright and sparkling;
compass them with love and light.
Fill, anoint them; send your Spirit,
holy dove and heart's delight.*

Ruth Duck
The United Methodist Hymnal, No. 605

Do you not know that all of us who have been baptized into Christ Jesus were baptized into his death? Therefore we have been buried with him by baptism into death, so that, just as Christ was raised from the dead by the glory of the Father, so we too might walk in newness of life. (Romans 6:3-4)

The church is formed by water and the Spirit into communities of disciples. In our baptism God claims us for the people of God, cleansing and incorporating us into the body of Christ. By our baptism we are bound in covenant with one another and with God to give witness to our new life in Christ.

Baptism is an outward and visible sign of God's action in calling out a chosen people. God divided the waters of creation to bring order and life out of chaos. God saved the chosen ones of Noah for an ark amid the flood. God delivered the people Israel by parting the waters of the Red Sea. So now by the waters of baptism God is claiming a new people to live for the reign of God.

Baptism is an outward and visible sign of that life in Christ to which faithful disciples give witness. Jesus himself stood in the Jordan to be baptized by John and rose up from those waters to bring healing and reconciliation to all who believed. Jesus sent his disciples out to invite and baptize others into the community of the new covenant. So now in the waters of baptism Christ is bringing new life to the church that gathers in his name.

Baptism is an outward and visible sign of an inward and spiritual grace. The Spirit blew across the waters of creation. The Spirit descended like a dove announcing the Sonship of Jesus Christ at his baptism. The Spirit came like a mighty wind and fiery flame to inspire the beginnings of the church. So now by the waters of baptism the Holy Spirit moves in the life of both the individual believer and the community of the faithful, bestowing the gifts needed to serve the reign of God.

Baptism is a sign of the life in Christ that is the spring of vitality in our congregations. Yet much to the detriment of our growing up in all ways into Christ (Ephesians 4:15), in many United Methodist congregations the full meaning of baptism is sorely neglected. If baptism is to be more than a sentimental ceremony, we must give greater attention to interpreting its meaning to candidates, their families, and the congregation itself.

The meaning of baptism is taught as much by how it is conducted as by sermons, books, or classes on the subject. The whole church can take joy in new forms that are coming into use such as gestures of pouring water into a bowl to heighten the water symbolism, and asking the congregation to reaffirm its faith alongside the candidates for baptism.

Since baptism of infants is practiced throughout United Methodism, its interpretation for both parents and congregation becomes even more important. United Methodists teach that in baptism God is acting to purify and claim the person for the covenant community. In turn it is the community's responsibility to help that person grow up into faith and discover her or his gifts of service to the Lord. During the ritual itself the worshipers join the parents or sponsors in affirming their faith in Jesus Christ and their commitment to discipleship.

Confirmation is the act in which the believer's gifts are called out and committed to the continuing ministry of Christ in the world. Confirmation is a critical opportunity for teaching, as adults and youth becoming adults consider their own faith and discipleship. Pastors and lay persons together must give full attention to this turning point in the lives of confirmands. The whole congregation joins the confirmands in remembering their baptism, so that baptism will be fresh in its claim on the lives of all.

Confirmation has sometimes been treated more as a rite of passage from puberty to adolescence than as an opportunity for teaching an inquiring person of any age. Confirmation has too often become a kind of "graduation from church," when it really marks the beginning point of learning, growth, and service.

Baptism, and its reaffirmation through the ritual of confirmation or at other times, is vital to congregations and the disciples who comprise them. Baptism is the basic sign of the Christian's vocation or calling in the

Every baptism reminds the people of Ozark First Church in Ozark, Alabama, of the baptism of a physically handicapped young adult and the loving response and welcome from the congregation.

This general ministry of all Christians in Christ's name and spirit is both a gift and a task. The gift is God's unmerited grace; the task is unstinting service. Entrance into the Church is acknowledged in Baptism and may include persons of all ages. In this Sacrament the Church claims God's promise, "the seal of the Spirit" (Ephesians 1:13). Baptism is followed by nurture and the consequent awareness by the baptized of the claim to ministry in Christ placed upon their lives by the Church. Such a ministry is ratified in confirmation, where the pledges of Baptism are accepted and renewed for life and mission. Entrance into and acceptance of ministry begin in a local church, but the impulse to minister always moves one beyond the congregation toward the whole human community. God's gifts are richly diverse for a variety of services; yet all have dignity and worth.
The Book of Discipline, 1988, ¶106

Will you diligently instruct the children in every place?
The Book of Discipline, 1988, ¶425:14

Each year at Central Church in Flint, Michigan, the confirmation class makes banners with which they parade into the sanctuary on the day they are confirmed.

Through confirmation,
and through the reaffirmation of our faith,
we renew the covenant declared at our baptism,
acknowledge what God is doing for us,
and affirm our commitment to Christ's holy church.
Baptismal Covenant I
The United Methodist Hymnal, page 33

VITAL CONGREGATIONS—FAITHFUL DISCIPLES

We share by water in his saving death.
Reborn, we share with him an Easter life
as living members of a living Christ.
Alleluia!

John Brownlow Geyer
The United Methodist Hymnal, No. 610

The baptismal font reminds members of Istrouma Church in Baton Rouge, Louisiana, of all the new life in their congregation—of babies and grandbabies baptized there.

Administered in obedience to our Lord, baptism is a sign and seal of our common discipleship. Through baptism, Christians are brought into union with Christ, with each other and with the Church of every time and place. Our common baptism, which unites us to Christ in faith, is thus a basic bond of unity. We are one people and are called to confess and serve one Lord in each place and in all the world.

Baptism, Eucharist, and Ministry
Faith and Order Commission
World Council of Churches

Through baptism
you are incorporated by the Holy Spirit
 into God's new creation
and made to share in Christ's royal priesthood.
We are all one in Christ Jesus.

Baptismal Covenant I
The United Methodist Hymnal, page 37

broadest sense, that "one hope" in which we have all been called (Ephesians 4:4). In baptism we die with Christ so that rising with him "we too might walk in newness of life" (Romans 6:4). "It is no longer I who live," wrote Paul, "but it is Christ who lives in me" (Galatians 2:20).

By the waters of baptism we enter into life "in Christ," in whom "there is a new creation: everything old has passed away; see, everything has become new!" (1 Corinthians 5:17). The old life is washed away and believers are pledged to God's kingdom, of which the resurrection of Jesus Christ is the first fruits (1 Peter 3:21). For in baptism we are adopted into the household of God, and become heirs of life eternal (Galatians 4:4-6).

In baptism we are also incorporated into the body of Christ. The baptized become part of a universal community, the people of the new covenant. Initiated into the family of God, the baptized find the role through which they can help to upbuild the whole body in love (Ephesians 4:16). The one Spirit aids each believer in finding a proper place in the body (1 Corinthians 12:13).

All the people of God, the whole *laos*, are called to ministry by virtue of being baptized. All baptized Christians are in full-time Christian service. All share the vocation of carrying on Christ's healing and reconciling ministry. And all have received by baptism the gifts they need to serve Christ in every walk of life, through school, work, civic activity, leisure, and home.

Vital congregations must make a regular and conscious effort to call out the gifts of their people. Many people do not realize the talents they have. Many have never seen a connection between their gift and their everyday activities. Many have not been challenged to put that gift to work for the mission of the church.

No task in the church is more important than the equipping or fitting together of the gifts of the people for the work of ministry (Ephesians 4:12). Congregations need to devote much time to training lay persons so that their gifts can be utilized in the service of Christ. Training gives people the background of a particular need, and the story of what else has been done about it. It gives them the information they need to carry out a task, and feedback on how they are doing once they have started. Training lets people know exactly what is expected and when. Overall it gives people a sense of strength in doing what they know how to do, and knowing that they are giving their best.

The ministries to which Christ calls the church are ministries for the whole people of God. Through their service, all the people give witness to their life in Christ. All of us are simply trying to follow where Jesus leads. And we can testify that anyone who seeks him can find him by joining in his ministry of reconciling love.

Membership in a Local Church

Having been "initiated into Christ's holy church," Christians also join themselves to a particular congregation and its tradition (such as United Methodism). Christian vocation is shapeless without participation in a specific congregation. Vital congregations worship together, recalling the story of Jesus and God's outreaching love. They study together to seek the meaning of discipleship today. They offer support and training so that members can be better able to serve Christ in daily life. Congregations provide believers with a community to which they can be accountable for their discipleship.

Therefore new members are asked to make a pledge of faithful participation in the ministries of the congregation, while current members renew their pledge with them. All commit (or recommit) their prayers, presence, gifts, and service to the ministries of that particular congregation. This commitment is not intended to confine Christian witness to the church building or church programs. A membership pledge does not limit the giving of money or time in the name of Christ only to the local or institutional church.

But through participation in the ministries of that particular congregation, members find definite ways to be personally involved. No one can serve the Lord in

The heart of Christian ministry is Christ's ministry of outreaching love. Christian ministry is the expression of the mind and mission of Christ by a community of Christians that demonstrates a common life of gratitude and devotion, witness and service, celebration and discipleship. All Christians are called to this ministry of servanthood in the world to the glory of God and for human fulfillment. The forms of this ministry are diverse in locale, in interest, and in denominational accent, yet always catholic in spirit and outreach.

The Book of Discipline, 1988, ¶104

Help us to be truly renewed that we may be the persons we were meant to be. Help us to be surprised by new visions of what it means to be the CHURCH where we are. May we respond to the winds of the spirit and reshape priorities. May we study for new understandings that will enable us to meet needs of each other and those whom we may touch. Help us to care about and to love both the lovely and the unlovely. We seek to be your true disciples. Amen.
Grace Church
Asheville, North Carolina

*As members of this congregation
will you faithfully participate in its ministries
   by your prayers, your presence,
   your gifts, and your service?*

I will.

Reception Into the Local Congregation
The United Methodist Hymnal, page 38

The hand carved baptismal font is a central and vital symbol for Community Church in Avondale, Arizona.

"The night my son tried to commit suicide, a member of the emergency medical team (who is also a member of our church) went to the Pastor's home. He told her what happened and she was at the hospital minutes later.

"She sat with my husband and me in the emergency room until late at night when the doctors told us our son would make it and we could go home.

"During that week she called on every member of the extended family (both grandmothers are in the congregation). The support and prayers I received from the church family (especially my 'Faith Sharing' group) were tremendous."

Monroe Church
Monroe, New York

Almighty God,
you have given us grace at this time
    with one accord to make our common supplication
        to you;
and you have promised through your well-beloved
        Son
    that when two or three are gathered together in his
        name,
    you will be in the midst of them.
Fulfill now, O Lord, our desire and petitions
    as may be best for us;
granting us in this world knowledge of your truth,
    and in the age to come life everlasting. Amen.

Prayer of John Chrysostom
The United Methodist Hymnal, No. 412

general, but only through specific, concrete actions. Local church congregations provide a structure for preparing and sending the people into their mission in everyday life.

Prayers

In pledging their prayers, people who enter into membership in a particular United Methodist congregation are binding themselves to a covenant of mutual prayer. In many congregations a prayer chain links all the members in spreading the word of a need or crisis in the local church family. The time of public prayers in worship begins with the naming of thanksgivings, cares, or concerns among the membership, which are then specifically brought before God.

In joining a local church, persons commit themselves to pray for others in that fellowship by name, knowing that they are being prayed for as well. Thus prayer is freed to move beyond preoccupation with one's own needs and difficulties. Prayer is stirred from the complacency of pleasant words uttered in vague generalities. Prayer becomes focussed on real people and real life situations.

At the same time, the local covenant of prayer is always joined with the prayers of all God's people everywhere. In asking God's healing graces for Mrs. Sanchez, whose pained face one can see, one is also joining prayers everywhere for the sick of every place who need God's kingdom promise of healing and wholeness. In asking God's consoling hope for Mr. Jones, whose unemployment and desperate circumstances one can see, one is also joining prayers everywhere for God's promised good news for the poor and those who hunger or thirst or suffer in any way.

Likewise, the pledge of prayers commits a local church member to regular participation in the public worship and prayer of the congregation. For through its gathered moments of song and silence, preaching and prayer, the whole congregation is strengthened and encouraged in mutual care. At the same time, the prayers of each local church are joined with the prayers of God's gathered people everywhere that the kingdom of God's healing, peace, justice and wholeness will come.

Presence

In pledging presence, a local church member is making a commitment to a spiritual discipline that is a companion to prayer. Presence is much more than a matter of being physically present. To be present is to be attentive, to pay attention, to be focussed on the people and activity where one is.

Contemporary life is busy, noisy, and full of distractions. Most of us live our lives scattered between home, market, workplace, school, and a myriad of other activities. The church is only one option among many ways to spend our time.

In the congregation we find a concrete place to focus and reflect on our lives. Here, in "reverent attendance upon the private and public worship of God," we can really pay attention to the needs of others. We can give our attention to the suffering and hope of people around the world. Here we can learn the discipline of being present.

In being present to others, centered on their joys and sorrows, we will also find others being present to us. In being present to God, paying attention to God's Word and giving attention to God's will for our lives, we also may know the presence of God.

Gifts

As baptized Christians, members of a local church congregation have already received many gifts with which to join in the ministry of the Lord. In pledging their gifts, they are making a commitment to know their own gifts and graces more clearly and to offer them in service.

One of the gifts of God's good creation is the gift of

One member of Mt. Vernon Church in Houston, Texas, recalls how some of the most significant turning points in her life occurred in church—her wedding, the baptism of her children, her daughter's wedding, her husband's funeral.

Each time a baptism occurs, we use a beautiful glass baptismal bowl. Sized to be held in two hands, it is clear glass shot through with deep blues, reds, and white. The bowl was hand-made and presented to our congregation by a man who had attended services there over a period of time. He was a life-long Buddhist who said, in leaving, that he had very much appreciated being a part of the community of our church but that, alas, we did "talk too much about Jesus."
Wallingford Church
Seattle, Washington

One of our members can "hug" you with her words. She loves the Lord and all people in the congregation. She is faithful.
Iglesia Evangelica de Co-op City
Bronx, New York

One member of our choir read in the paper that a hundred-member choir from Ghana had arrived in Nashville a week early for a series of concerts in local churches. After further investigation, we discovered that the local churches had not formally agreed to sponsor the concerts. After several telephone calls, our congregation launched into responding to the needs of the Ghana group by providing food, transportation, housing, and concert opportunities.
Clark Memorial Church
Nashville, Tennessee

VITAL CONGREGATIONS—FAITHFUL DISCIPLES

The collection plates used to be entirely metal and change (which was the main contribution in the early days) "clanged" as the plate was passed. Often the plate stopped as some members made change before passing the plate on down the pew. The children watched certain people whom they knew were likely to make change.

First Church
Bluefield, Virginia

*Take my life, and let it be
consecrated, Lord, to thee.
Take my moments and my days;
let them flow in ceaseless praise.
Take my hands, and let them move
at the impulse of thy love.
Take my feet, and let them be
swift and beautiful for thee.*

*Take my voice, and let me sing
always, only, for my King.
Take my lips, and let them be
filled with messages from thee.
Take my silver and my gold;
not a mite would I withhold.
Take my intellect, and use
every power as thou shalt choose.*

Frances R. Havergal
The United Methodist Hymnal, No. 399

material resources. Like other gifts, these resources are pledged to the upbuilding of the body in love. Congregations cannot function without them. At the same time, congregations are only the conduit through which Christian disciples give their resources to support ministries in Christ's name throughout the world.

Giving, too, is a discipline of the spirit, in response to God's Word. The biblical standard of giving is the tithe, the gift of a tenth of one's material resources to God's purposes as guided by the community of faith. Tithing was a sign of belonging to the covenant community in ancient Israel and throughout our tradition. So today the tithe indicates our joining in a covenant of ministry not only in our congregations, but in our connection that stretches around the world.

United Methodists are continually challenged by John Wesley's principles of giving. "Render unto God," Wesley preached, "not a tenth, not a third, not half, but all that is God's, be it more or less." By this he meant that all money in excess of what is necessary to keep oneself and one's family at a reasonable standard of living, all money beyond provision of necessities, is to be given away. The determination of what is necessary is a matter of individual conscience, for each person has to give an account of his or her stewardship before God.

To be able to give away all but what we need is to be free to live for God's purposes. It is to be master of our material belongings in a world obsessed with acquiring and consuming things. In Christian giving we achieve a detachment from what we own in order to possess those things that we cannot own: love for others, sympathy for the plight of those who suffer, and freedom to help people in need.

Service

Through congregations, disciples of Christ find concrete ways to put their gifts to work in the service of the Lord. They join in what the New Testament church called *diakonia*, the ministry of visiting the sick, comforting the afflicted, helping the poor. This ministry has typified the church from the beginning and therefore is part of what makes the church the church.

Jesus Christ called people, after all, not first to any form of ritual or statement of beliefs. He called them to follow, and when they followed, they found themselves touching lepers and visiting with prisoners, feeding hungry people and calling out the demons preventing others from fullness of life.

Vital congregations direct their members into forms of service that follow after Christ. They help people identify their special gift, and offer them an opportunity to put it to work in service. In their commitment and involvement in a particular place, members are joined with the company of disciples everywhere who give witness to Christ's ministry of reconciling love.

All the vows of membership in a local church congregation grow out of and put into concrete expression the baptism of every Christian. Therefore congregations must regularly celebrate the reaffirmation of baptism. This is not to be understood as re-baptism, or baptism performed over again. Rather it is a remembering of one's baptism by water and the Spirit given once and for all.

Through the constant remembering of the larger context of baptism, the congregation can prevent its understanding of church membership from being reduced to the forms of any other association, club, or social group. Presence will not be reduced to a registration list. Gifts will not be reduced to dues paid the organization.

In the full context of baptism, church membership becomes an outward expression of the whole life of Christian discipleship. In renewing our baptismal covenant, we are recalled to the vocation that encompasses and transforms every aspect of our lives. Vital congregations are full of people with "wet hair," whose baptisms are fresh. For our baptism gives us our most fundamental vocation: to live in the hope of God's new creation.

Wesley Church is in the city of Olongapo, The Philippines, where the largest US naval base outside the United States is located. The church not only ministers to its two thousand members and people from the base, but also reaches out to the hospitality girls through a community center that provides rehabilitation services, skills retraining, and health and medical facilities.

"The baptismal font means a lot to me because, when my child was baptized there, we rededicated ourselves to doing something with the rest of our lives. I have wet-eyed memories."
Covenant Church
Dothan, Alabama

Come, let us use the grace divine,
and all with one accord,
in a perpetual covenant join
ourselves to Christ the Lord;
give up ourselves, thru Jesus' power,
his name to glorify;
and promise, in this sacred hour,
for God to live and die.
Charles Wesley
The United Methodist Hymnal, No. 606

PRAYERS OF THE CONGREGATION

As a community of people seeking together the salvation of the Lord and journeying together toward God's reign, we bring our prayers before God.

We have heard the Word that God is the fountain of life; we have heard Jesus' promise that whoever drinks of the water Christ gives will never be thirsty again. We come now to dip into that well, praying that the Holy Spirit may give us words to say that express the deepest needs of ourselves and of others.

We trust that prayer opens to us a vista of God's intentions for us and for our world. We trust that in prayer we receive the perspectives and insights we need, through which the Spirit inspires vision for the church.

For the Spirit to stir in us new vision
    above all else
        we pray.

VITAL CONGREGATIONS—FAITHFUL DISCIPLES

*Prayer is the soul's sincere desire,
unuttered or expressed,
the motion of a hidden fire
that trembles in the breast.*

*Prayer is the Christians' vital breath,
the Christians' native air;
their watchword at the gates of death;
they enter heaven with prayer.*

*O Thou, by whom we come to God,
the Life, the Truth, the Way:
the path of prayer thy self hast trod;
Lord, teach us how to pray!*

James Montgomery
The United Methodist Hymnal, No. 492

One person mentioned the importance of the altar rail. He appreciated that ours is a kneeling church. He often comes in during the week and kneels and prays in solitude.

Woodbine Church
Woodbine, Kansas

*Sweet hour of prayer! sweet hour of prayer!
thy wings shall my petition bear
to him whose truth and faithfulness
engage the waiting soul to bless.
And since he bids me seek his face,
believe his word, and trust his grace,
I'll cast on him my every care,
and wait for thee, sweet hour of prayer!*

William Walford
The United Methodist Hymnal, No. 496

Rejoice always, pray without ceasing, give thanks in all circumstances; for this is the will of God in Christ Jesus for you. (1 Thessalonians 5:16-18)

Christian congregations are communities of prayer. Through the corporate prayers of worship, through prayers at times of fellowship and study, and through the prayers of faithful disciples, congregations are united in supplication to God.

All prayer is communal; for it is one God to whom we lift our petitions. Whether we pray as a corporate body or as individuals, our prayers for one another bind us into one communion. Indeed our prayers unite us with all the faithful of every age in one communion of the saints.

Prayer is a sign of vitality in the congregation, for prayer is fed by the living stream that flows from Christ. We pray in words that Jesus taught his disciples to say. We also discover, as Jesus taught us by example, that prayer undergirds every moment of our ministry on behalf of the Kingdom.

Prayer precedes, underlies, feeds, and refreshes the ministry and mission of the congregation. Through prayer we drink from the wellspring of God's love and healing, and are given vision and courage for our work.

Prayer is a sign of who we believe God is; for our prayers are to God made known to us in Jesus Christ. We pray to God whose covenant of love draws us into faithfulness, and on whom we make this claim: Keep your promises, O God, and fulfill your reign of wholeness, love, and justice as you have promised. This is our prayer.

Prayer is a sign that we are serious about the intentions of God to whom we pray. In asking that God's kingdom come, we are declaring our willingness to be changed, to become a new people. For when God's promises are kept, there is a new creation, and nothing can be the same as it was before. Thus we ask first for the courage to pray, and to pray as we ought, knowing that when our prayers are heard, we will have challenges and sacrifices ahead of us.

Let us then bring our petitions to God, in confidence

PRAYERS OF THE CONGREGATION

that what is impossible to us is possible with God.

Let us pray for the needs of others and of our world, knowing that God will call us to intercede ourselves in deeds of love.

Let us pray for those outside the faith and fellowship of the church, that all may know the love of God made known in Jesus Christ.

Let us pray for one another, as congregations of faithful disciples seeking vitality in Christ, that we may be effective in the mission to which God calls us.

Let us uphold one another in prayer across the United Methodist connection, that we may be united in purpose and sustained in our hope.

Let us pray that whether we are assembled as congregations or dispersed into every walk of life, we will be blessed through the patterns of prayer with a constant sense of God's holy presence.

Let us pray that God will bless us with living water, welling up like a spring within us, giving us life and life abundantly.

"When the minister comes down the aisles, asking for prayer concerns, people stand up and share with the rest of us their joys and their sorrows. We respond: 'Hear our prayer, O Lord.' I feel a oneness with God and with others present during this time."
Bear Creek Church
Houston, Texas

My prayer rises to heaven, to the mystery of God's power,
as the smoke ascends when the precious incense burns.
Have mercy on us, Lord, and grant us your grace.
My voice glorifies the Lord God of majesty,
as the night bird sings at the dawning of the day.
This is my offering to God, the Lord of all.
Dao Kim
The United Methodist Hymnal, No. 498

Nguyen D. Viet-Chan, Publisher-Editor; Dan Chua Catholic Magazine & Publications; P.O. Box 1419; Gretna, LA 70053.

God does nothing except in response to prayer.
John Wesley

As Congregations of the Faithful, We Offer These Prayers for the Church

Almighty God,
We are surrounded in this place
by the signs, the symbols
and the literal expressions of strength and history.

The stones of the building
stand graceful, but firm
Reminding us that
the men and women who preceded us
looked far beyond their own needs;
that they sacrificed
for the future;
and that the faithfulness of their dreams
have stood the test of time.

Our inheritance is all around us—
beauty, endurance, stability, strength.

Our inheritance is all around us—
giving us sanctuary, peace, shelter,
and a firm foundation
upon which to build and sustain
a community of faith.

We pray, Oh God,
that we will use that foundation,
or find the comforts of personal faith,
not merely as a place of rest
but as a *point d'appui* [of departure]
from which to serve the world.

Not merely as a place to hide
from harsh realities,
but as a vantage point
from which to share
the address of faith
for human life.

PRAYERS OF THE CONGREGATION

Our inheritance is all around us—
but now
we are the ones who fill the pews,
the board meetings,
the commissions and committees.

We are the ones
who face the challenges,
the decisions,
the directions.

We are the ones
who dream the dreams,
not just for ourselves,
but for our
children's, children's, children.

We pray then, for our church
not a new prayer,
but the timeless one
that Jesus prayed for those first disciples;
that we may be one
so that the world might believe in God's presence,
that we might reflect God's glory
so that the world might see God's love,
that we may seek perfection
so that the world may know in whose name we act.

We pray for our church
the strength of the old,
and the joy of the new,
the security of the past,
the compelling lure of the future.

In the name of the one
who prayed for us
and first taught us to pray.

from the poetry of Beverly Sawyer
First United Methodist Church
Hot Springs, Arkansas

Dear God,
We are truly grateful for the many gifts, graces, and talents that we find in our church. We are thankful that the spirit of your servant, the Christ, dwells among us. Where we have served you well, bless our efforts, and where we have fallen short, increase our vision.

First Church
Sabetha, Kansas

Lord, revitalize and renew us in the Spirit. Open our hearts and minds for new visions and new perspectives. In the midst of our struggles and hard work, help us never lose sight of your promise that your grace is sufficient for us. Charge us up by your Spirit, and let us deeply trust in your justice and mercy. Let each moment pass by with high awareness of your presence with us.

Chinese Community Church
Oakland, California

O God, we praise you for your bountiful blessings.
For the love received and given,
   we give you thanks.
For the work and dedication of members of your family,
   we thank you.
For the new and beautiful facilities, remembering the sacrifices of many,
   we praise your name.

Give us insights to the needs of others and show us ways to fulfill those needs. Guide us to be an open, receptive, welcoming Church. Help us to live and grow in Christ, to love, and to learn to live with others and to worship in peace and brotherhood/sisterhood.

Support us as we seek to be the Body of Christ not only within our Church, but in the community and the world. Unify our different parts, so that we might show forth that love which binds us and that sends us forth to be missionaries for Christ.

Guilford College Church
Greensboro, North Carolina

PRAYERS OF THE CONGREGATION

Awaken us, dear Lord.
Help us to be more like Jesus.
Give us new visions and energy.
Help make us good stewards of our many blessings.
Replace our hindsight with foresight.
Unite us in faithfulness to your will, for your glory.
St. Luke's Church
Kokomo, Indiana

Gracious Lord, Who has brought us to where we are and cares for each one of us, grant that we may be more fully dedicated to continue together as your church. While not forgetting the past but anticipating the future with hope, grant that we may grow in personal relationship within the church and remain open to new people.
OmakRiverside Church
Omak, Washington

Dear God,
Help us to be a more caring and warm congregation. Bless our church and our members. Create within us the desire to be better Christians. Help us to be dedicated and hard-working, and help us to have a strong commitment to our church and to our responsibilities as Christians. We ask a special blessing for the people who do not feel comfortable in our congregation. We ask that they would feel the warmness that radiates within our congregation and that they would feel a part of our family. Above all, we ask that the work we do will be acceptable in thy sight.
Central Church
Atlanta, Georgia

Hear our cry for salvation, for peace at home and for peace in the world. Turn our cannons into flower pots, sustain us in fulfilling your/our missions. May our voices and hearts be continually lifted in song. Help us discern the important things in life, and give us the strength to do them. Establish our priorities. Keep alive our concerns for others. Thank you for those who gave us guidance in the past; we pray for wisdom in the future.

VITAL CONGREGATIONS—FAITHFUL DISCIPLES

Help us to truly believe that you provide for us, and answer our prayers when we pray, "give us this day our daily bread." May we have an abiding faith and enduring love for each other.

The United Methodist Church
Palmyra, Missouri

Thank you Lord for your constant witness in the hearts and lives of many individuals in this congregation. Continue to make this attitude and spiritual core grow, to attract others, that they too may witness for you. Help us not to be proud. Teach us to disagree in love. We can't imagine our potential to bring your kingdom here on earth. Help us to be open to your leading in what we do that it may be to your glory, that our church can become what you would have us be.

Asbury Church
Madison, Wisconsin

Lord, let us be what you want us to be—say and do what you want.
Let us love one another as you have loved us.
Let us accept the challenges. May we offer ourselves unconditionally.
What God has done for us, let us do for others.
Let us pray about negative attitudes.

First Church
Batesville, Mississippi

Dear God,
We thank you for this church and its members. Those of us who have been here for many years are aware of the constant love and care you have shown us, especially in the last few days since we have been struck by fire. We thank you for that, and pray that you will continue to bestow your blessings on this congregation and the work we are doing and will be doing in the months to come. Open our eyes and hearts to further service for your

PRAYERS OF THE CONGREGATION

people and grant us the strength and courage to do your will and follow your way.

Wesley Church
Framingham, Massachusetts

God, make us relevant. Help us to see the needs of others and make it possible for your response to those needs to be expressed through the ministry of this church. Help us to go on doing the things we do right and to be willing to change when change is necessary. Keep us strong and healthy.

St. Paul's Church
Lawton, Michigan

O God of love and power, grace and beauty, we adore you and give praise to you for all of the blessings that contribute to our existence. In this attitude of gratitude and thankfulness, may we see the possibilities to make disciples of all people.

May our joy send us into the world, telling our neighbors and our friends about your loving kindness, that they too may witness that your presence is in this place. Thank you for your living spirit that gives us the wisdom to be a growing church. May our membership growth reflect our inner commitment to let the light you have given us shine before all people.

Clark Memorial Church
Nashville, Tennessee

Dear God,
We pray that we may stay open to your way for us
—that as we grow stronger in Christ, that we grow more like him in ministry and mission;
—that we may grow not only in numbers but in social witness.

Hazardville Church
Enfield, Connecticut

Dear God,
This is the group of Christians with whom I have chosen to worship and work together for your Kingdom. May we be a people of vision. May we reach out to the

hurting. May we always have an open mind towards new ideas, new ways of worship. May we continue to care as we grow. May we have honest communication and always look to Thy word for our guidance.

Pioneer Church
Walla Walla, Washington

O God, we pray that we will be a group of people who are enabled by your Holy Spirit to pray without ceasing and serve you with gladness. Help us to be constantly aware of your presence and our place in your kingdom. Enable us to do your Word in the world. We also pray that you will help us discover how we can make all people feel at home in our congregation. Guide us to those whom you would have us to serve in your name and bring into the fellowship of our church.

First Church
Lawndale, North Carolina

Lord, help our church to be more aware of all you have already given us. Guide us to assist others. Help us to ease the pain and grief of others. Help us to reach out even further into our community. Let our bodies and minds come to rest and our hearts open to hear you. Give us then the courage to respond with our lives to serve you.

Christ Church
Rockford, Illinois

Dear Lord,
Help us in our daily lives as we make contact with others to extend a sense of caring and respect. We know that even just a smile can make a difference. Help us to grow strong in body and mind, and teach us to relax and take time out to "smell the roses" in this world which seems to be going so fast. Help us to set our priorities as to what is important in our lives. Help each one of us as your stewards to go forth and spread your love and your strength so that those who do not know you will be able to learn more about you through our commitment.

Ripley Church
Dexter, Maine

PRAYERS OF THE CONGREGATION

Give us knowledge, Lord, make us realize what we have at our fingertips within our community and world.

Help us to overcome our lethargy and preoccupation with ourselves, so that we can see beyond ourselves to the needs of others. Let us open our circle to include those who are left outside. Strengthen and inspire us to serve you every day of our lives.

With all people everywhere, we pray.

First Church
Winfield, Kansas

Dear Lord,
Help us to each use our talents to the fullest,
provide us with good health,
help us to communicate with one another and not go off
   on our own,
help us to try not to be discouraged and to be aware of
   our self-worth,
and help us to continue to be a loving and caring
   congregation.

Christ Church
Salisbury, Maryland

O Jesus, save us from professionalism, from the smooth phrase and the slick word. Make us real—real in action, word, and deed. Give us humble hearts and receptive faith. Then we shall live by your simplicities.

St. Paul Church
Clinton, Mississippi

Dear God,
We thank you for the love and the fellowship that we know through thy Son, and through this church. Make us more aware of our responsibility as your representatives in the place where we find ourselves. Help us to be willing servants in the work of thy kingdom. Bless the efforts of our congregation as we seek to share the love we know from Thee.

Central Trinity Church
Zanesville, Ohio

VITAL CONGREGATIONS—FAITHFUL DISCIPLES

Lead us in the path we must follow.
May we seek members not to grow, but to love.
May we build buildings not for space, but for learning.
May we grasp a sense of your mission, O Lord, and
    through the grace you have given in Christ, may we
    persevere to its end.

Skidaway Island Church
Savannah, Georgia

Lord, help us to be more loving. Walk with us and help us to reach out to others. Keep us from being weary in well-doing. Help us to continue to grow, not only mentally, but spiritually and to make a commitment to our youth program. Let us have vision and forgive us our shortcomings. We ask these things in the name of Jesus.

Trinity Church
Sequim, Washington

God, we are the product of a local community Christian tradition. It wears well on us and those around us. Help us to survive and pull our young with us into the coming times.

Ebenezer Church
Newberry, South Carolina

Lord Jesus, keep Jack's Creek in your love, and help us all be faithful to our calling to be your faithful people, and bring us all to heaven to share eternity with you.

Jack's Creek Church
Roark, Kentucky

PRAYERS OF THE CONGREGATION

O holy and loving God,
    We lift our hearts and voices in praise of You, our Creator, Redeemer, Sustainer and Friend.
    We marvel at the splendor of your creation.
    We are awed by the boundlessness of your redeeming love.
    We are overwhelmed by the daily gifts with which you sustain our lives.
    We rejoice in your continuing presence with us through your Holy Spirit.
    In praise and adoration we sing with the Psalmist, "Bless the Lord, O my soul, and all that is within me, bless God's holy name."

O God of grace,
    Through our baptism you have included us in the church. You have shown to us through Jesus and his disciples in every age your will for the community of faith. Forgive us for our failure to follow Him who denied self and went the way of servanthood that led him to a cross. Grant, O God, that each of us might remember daily our baptism and, remembering, make a fresh surrender of life to Christ.
    Through our sharing in Holy Communion you give to us your Holy Spirit. Forgive us for our neglect of this sacrament. Draw us to that table, we pray, where you wait to empower us for life and mission.

O God of mercy and power,
    We, who have been called and set apart for the office of bishop in the church, pray for your daily guidance as we seek to serve. Forgive us for those times when we have failed to fulfill our calling. Enable us, we pray, by the power of your Holy Spirit indwelling us, to be good teachers of your truth, to hold ever before the church your vision for vital congregational life, to use the resources of our office to encourage laity and clergy in mission, and to call your people to lives of physical and spiritual discipline by our words and example.

VITAL CONGREGATIONS—FAITHFUL DISCIPLES

We pray for all laity and clergy in every land who serve as ministers of Jesus Christ.

Bless with your grace those who serve as pastors of local congregations. Give to them a fresh experience each day of your presence and power.

We thank you for those laypersons who demonstrate faithful discipleship in their daily activities and vocational pursuits. Enrich, we pray, their congregational life and bless the church that resides in the house of each one of them.

O God of the covenant,

You have commissioned us to go and make disciples of all people and to bring them by baptism into covenant with you. As individual disciples and as local congregations we accept this commission. We pray that you will guard and sustain by your love all who serve in this mission of your redeeming grace.

O God of hope,

We thank you that we can face the future with the assurance that You, who have given to us in Jesus a vision for your church, will give to those who will receive it the wisdom, courage, faith and faithfulness to make it a reality. In that confidence we dedicate ourselves to the vision of vital congregational life and faithful discipleship.

We offer our prayer in the name of Jesus Christ, our living Lord. *Amen.*

The Council of Bishops
The United Methodist Church

OFFERING OUR RESPONSE TO THE LORD

God's vision for the church has come to us through the Word. We have reaffirmed our covenant commitment to that vision through baptism. We have sought through our prayers a deeper discernment of that vision and of God's purposes for us.

Now the time has come for us to offer ourselves, all that we have and all that we are, in the witness and service of the Lord. We now present to God the actions and qualities of our lives that are signs of our life in Christ.

Some of what we offer expresses the work that only congregations can do through the dynamic interaction of vitality and faithfulness in the community of believers. Some of what we offer expresses personal commitments for which we individually take responsibility.

We pray that all our gifts will be to the glory of God, as signs that point to the vision of God's reign that is our hope.

VITAL CONGREGATIONS—FAITHFUL DISCIPLES

Whenever Jesus is in the center, we can see the effects, not only in our church, but also in other denominations. By evangelization, adoration services, and open meetings in private houses (we have about ten groups of people meeting regularly in private houses), we encourage people who do not yet belong to our congregation to join us.

The United Methodist Church
Schönaich, West Germany

*Bless thou the gifts our hands have brought;
bless thou the work our hearts have planned.
Ours is the faith, the will, the thought;
the rest, O God, is in thy hand.*

Samuel Longfellow
The United Methodist Hymnal, No. 587

The church of Jesus Christ, in the power and unity of the Holy Spirit, is called to serve as an alternative community to an alienated and fractured world: a loving and peaceable international company of disciples transcending all governments, races and ideologies, reaching out to all "enemies," ministering to all the victims of poverty and oppression. To be an alternative community is not to withdraw from worldly affairs; it is to be at once a model of humane relationships and a base for social transformation.

The Council of Bishops
Foundation Document,
In Defense of Creation

You did not choose me but I chose you. And I appointed you to go and bear fruit, fruit that will last, so that the Father will give you whatever you ask him in my name. I am giving you these commands so that you may love one another. (John 15:16-17)

Fed by the streams of life in Christ, Christians as individuals and as congregations grow up into faith. Like healthy trees with roots stretching to the river of life (Psalm 80:11), they bear the fruit of their relationship with Jesus Christ. For Christ is their light and their salvation, the fountain of life (Psalm 36:9) by which they are healed and fed. Through him they are strengthened to bear that water of abundant life for others.

Life in Christ takes many forms in congregations and in individual disciples. No single way of being a vital congregation, no one form of faithful discipleship can apply to everyone in all times and places. In fact, to assert only one way would itself stifle the very life we seek. No two congregations can respond to the demands of discipleship in exactly the same ways.

The general church or the Council of Bishops cannot advocate "ten steps" toward vitality in congregations, or "eight ways" to be a faithful disciple. No grid of absolutes can be overlaid on the living organisms of our congregations. Our connectional covenant is not suited to the management of grand master plans.

Our covenant does sustain a lively network of mutual concern in which our multiple signs of vitality and faithfulness are celebrated. Bearing each other's burdens and sharing each other's joys, congregations yoked together in conference relationships continually praise God for the signs of life in Christ that are evident in each other's work. Neither imposing their "successes" on each other, nor hiding their "failures," they can freely support each other's ministries and pray for God to open new avenues of mission in each place. They can challenge each other to see and respond to those avenues in the unique way each is gifted to do.

The signs described below point toward Christ's ministry being active through congregational mission and personal discipleship. These signs will take a unique form in any given congregation, and in any believer.

This is not a checklist for "keeping score" and measuring just how vital one's congregation really is. It is not a laundry list of expectations. Neither does it represent a lowest common denominator allowing one to say, "I do one of these things, therefore I know I am faithful." Rather these are expressions of the life of Christ within us, a life which we seek with unflagging commitment and continual self-examination.

The signs are interactive as well. Congregations form and equip disciples; disciples bring their gifts to the life of the congregation and extend its ministries to the everyday world. Neither exists without the other. Each is an element in the chemistry that makes each congregation especially able to fulfill its calling as a people of God in a particular place.

Signs of Vitality in Congregational Life

Worshiping in a Way that Calls People to Conversion and Commitment

The people who "come to church" for worship are in many different states of mind and stages of life. They come complete with all their longings and their doubts, their questions and their certainties. They come both shaken in their trust and confident in their hopes. They come above all to find out, "Can I put my faith in this Jesus for the meaning of life and of death? Is there truly hope here for the salvation of the world?" Given life in Christ, a vital congregation answers with a resounding yes. In Christ there is hope, for Christ reveals God as One who embraces a hurting world with the divine love.

In vital congregations all who worship there can sense the reality of God. The service conveys a spirit of awe, and the people know that they stand in the presence of a wonderful mystery. This does not mean that everyone is equally convicted of his or her own failings and need of grace, nor that all will experience God's presence. No

Worship is both the core of life together and the main entry point for new people. We have a very modern-looking sanctuary that seats 100 people. Our worship style fits our worship space and the relaxed Malibu lifestyle. There is an informality—a feeling of family gathering together. Everyone is known and visitors often comment on how quickly they feel "at home." The warmth is genuine, as especially evidenced in the sharing of joys and concerns at prayer time. We are known for our image-filled liturgy and contemporary music. We use piano (no organ) plus electronic keyboard; only a small portion of our congregational music comes from the Hymnal. There is a variety of sermon styles, including bimonthly original dramatic sermons or plays. Because of the pastoral team, our worship necessarily reflects a balance of male and female.

The contemporary worship has drawn a young congregation that increased by fifty percent in two and a half years. We have now had a plateau year in which those members were more fully assimilated and the church adjusted to its growth. At seventy members, we are still a small church in membership but our program and staffing reflect a commitment on the part of members and staff to offer Christ in new and exciting ways.

Anne Broyles, Pastor
Malibu Church
Malibu, California

We find that singing is one of the most important parts of the church service and like songs that are uplifting—not sad and slow. We still like the old hymns better but are willing to try some of the new.

OmakRiverside Church
Omak, Washington

Usually once a week each of these groups (Latin American Christian Base Communities) joins for biblical reflection and celebration. Ordinarily a trained lay leader takes the lead of the group. These meetings combine Biblical reflection with prayers and song (celebration); occasionally the Eucharist is served when a clergy is available.

These meetings have three parts: to see, to judge, to act. To see: An analysis and/or a testimony of a given concrete social, political or economic issue among the poor; to judge: A biblical reflection in correlation with the previous analysis or testimony; to act: A definition of the pastoral lines to follow, organization of communal tasks.

It is in this way that the Bible is appropriated by the poor. They feel interpreted and challenged by God's Word to become poor in spirit in terms of their own historical liberation. Thus the Scripture becomes the Bible of the poor.

Jorge Pantelis, Pastor
Calvary Church
Washington, D.C.

Our church has changed. We are more open. It used to be that people from the "projects" felt uncomfortable in our church and our church people possibly felt uncomfortable with them. But now they come to church and unite with our church and everyone is happy.

First Church
Livingston, Tennessee

single experience of conversion is present to all. Yet the whole congregation unites in song and prayer, seeking the God to whose power the saints of all the ages testify.

Singing the hymns of the church is a wellspring of vitality in United Methodist congregations. Through uplifted voice and the images of poetry, people join in a common language of God and God's salvation. Even the skeptic is moved when a thousand tongues sing the Redeemer's praise. Many of our congregations have already eagerly received the new United Methodist hymnal. This is a book of songs drawn from many streams of testimony to God's grace. These hymns and prayers will give voice to the faith and hope of contemporary believers.

Hearing the Word of God for today is at the heart of vitality in a congregation. Yet we all too rarely open the Bible. We remember, understand, and apply its stories and images of faith all too little. No preaching or other worship action can take place today with the assumption that the people in the pews know anything about Abraham or Ruth, the teachings of Jesus or the writings of Paul.

Having Bibles available for all worshipers is one way of involving people in reading Scripture. If the congregation follows the lectionary, or calendar of Bible readings for each Sunday of the year, people will have a taste of many different biblical traditions. Worship leaders can plan services around the themes of those readings, thus deepening their meaning for worshipers.

Preaching that is firmly grounded in Scripture and its interpretation for today's questions of discipleship is a sign of life in Christ. Scriptural preaching disciplines both preacher and hearer to pay attention to the story of God's love and justice revealed in the Bible. All of our pressing current needs are thus placed in a larger perspective that calls us out of ourselves into the service of Christ.

People are hungry for the Word of God's love and forgiveness. People want to hear the call to discipleship. And how will they hear without a preacher (Romans 10:14)? The training and preparation of preachers is critically important today. Mass communications have altered the attention span and expectations of many listeners. Yet people continue to be drawn to sermons grounded in Scripture and preached with passion and imagination.

Preaching and worship in vital congregations calls people to conversion, to a new way of looking at the world, to a turning around of all their accustomed patterns of thinking and living. Our preaching and worship must challenge with the power and promise of God's transforming presence the assumptions of a world rushing on as if God did not exist. In our worship we give testimony to the power of God to heal, to reconcile, to bring justice, even in an unbelieving world. We convey our sense of mystery and awe as we stand before the maker of heaven and earth, God our Creator, Redeemer, and Sustainer.

Celebrating the Sacraments Regularly

Vital congregations regularly celebrate the sacraments of baptism and Holy Communion, with interpretation of their meaning. The rituals in the new hymnal greatly increase the congregation's participation in the sacraments and provide much more opportunity for conveying their meaning. The spectator quality of sacramental "performance" is diminishing in favor of greater involvement from all worshipers.

When the water of baptism is poured into the font, or flows by in the river, all of us are reminded of our own baptism. We are all refreshed in our vocation of continuing Christ's ministry. We are renewed as a people of God, and given new gifts by the power of the Holy Spirit through the new person's incorporation into the family.

The power of Holy Communion as a means of grace is attested in the actions of Jesus himself and in the testimony of the whole church. John Wesley made regular attendance at the Lord's Supper a minimum requirement for Methodist people. At the Table Christ has promised his presence. In bread and cup we are joined with Christ and with one another in the promise of salvation.

God of the sparrow
God of the whale
God of the swirling stars
How does the creature say Awe
How does the creature say Praise

God of the neighbor
God of the foe
God of the pruning hook
How does the creature say Love
How does the creature say Peace

God of the ages
God near at hand
God of the loving heart
How do your children say Joy
How do your children say Home

Jaroslav J. Vajda
The United Methodist Hymnal, No. 122

Text Copyright © 1983, Jaroslav J. Vajda. All rights reserved. Used by permission.

During the last eighteen months, we have experimented with some changes in our baptismal liturgy, using the more ancient formulas more frequently and we have also introduced intinction as a method for receiving communion. Many of our people feel that this has encouraged the church to focus more deeply on the meaning of the sacraments for our corporate life.

Northbrook Church
Roswell, Georgia

A lady from a local home for mentally retarded adults called about two years ago looking for a church where the handicapped could receive communion even though they were not members or might not understand communion well. We welcomed them, and they have been coming ever since.

The Church of Hastings
Hastings, Minnesota

VITAL CONGREGATIONS—FAITHFUL DISCIPLES

A member of the Church of All Nations in Boston, Massachusetts, was involved in a tragic crime that drew a lot of media coverage. Throughout the investigation and trial, church members supported the family with cards, letters, gifts, love, and prayer.

We live in an era when the identity and mission of the church has been buffeted and challenged from all sides. In the past similar experiences led to intensified commitments to education for the sake of the continuity and relevance of the community's faith. Out of the depths of the exile, the Jews created the synagogue to ensure the instruction of future generations. As an oppressed minority people, the early church developed the catechumenate [education for new Christians based on the creeds] to build up the body of Christ. In the intellectual chaos of the middle ages monasteries and universities preserved ancient teachings and began the long process of attempting to make sense out of the church's Hebrew, Greek, and Roman roots for contemporary life and faith.

The Wesleys organized bands and societies with the intent of creating communities of faith in the byways of industrial England. In the arbors of many plantations African American Christians rehearsed the stories of the Bible, sang hymns of lament and praise, and incorporated subsequent generations into rituals of prayer and exhortation. During the nineteenth century the Sunday school was adapted to the task of extending a Christian civilization into the American wilderness. And in many of the so-called "growing churches" today, congregational life has been reordered around the deliberate and systematic exposition of scripture to guide daily life in a secular world.

Charles R. Foster, Professor
Candler School of Theology
Atlanta, Georgia

We neglect the sacraments at our peril, for without them our congregations' proclamation of the gospel is reduced to our words only. Through the sacraments the power of Christ is present to the people of God in ways that we can never convey through mere words.

Forming Disciples

Vital congregations shape the lives of participants in the beliefs and values that make the Christian life distinctive. They are not content to let social expectations of the "good person" be the definition of Christian discipleship. They encourage people to center themselves around life in Christ through Scripture, growth in faith, and spiritual discipline.

An active and growing Sunday school for people of all ages sparks vitality. For congregations are among the few places, at least in Western societies, in which people gather across generational lines as a family of faith. We learn from one another as we hear the questions of faith and the challenges of Scripture. We encourage each other in Christian discipleship for everyday living.

Vital congregations provide many opportunities for study for people of all ages. Pastors teach the Scriptures and take a primary role as teacher of teachers. Leaders are continually forming small groups and classes to bring people together for discussion and to provide points of entry for new members. Not confined to Sunday mornings, these opportunities are tailored to the schedules and needs of participants.

The topics and materials for Christian education in vital congregations are deeply rooted in Scripture and in Christian tradition. The stories and images of the faithful across the centuries spur us to seek appropriate forms of the life of faith today.

Vital congregations offer patterns for growth in spiritual life and discipline. The whole congregation may follow a daily lectionary or set of Bible readings to be studied privately through the week. Small groups may be formed around a covenant of mutual prayer. Services of morning and evening prayer may be provided as a structure for beginning and ending each day.

OFFERING OUR RESPONSE TO THE LORD

The Wesleyan tradition gives us a compelling model for spiritual growth. John Wesley built a framework of discipline that included daily prayer and Scripture reading, regular attendance upon Holy Communion, and fasting so that the money saved could be given to the poor. In vital congregations the people use these means as a structure for growth in Christ, through which the whole body is built up in its witness.

Practicing Care and Hospitality

The fellowship meal, long a favorite activity in congregations, is a symbol of the whole caring nature of the community of faith given life in Christ. Vital congregations are communities of hospitality, offering open space in which people can find a place at the table. People learn to share one another's joys and sorrows, to help one another think through decisions and responsibilities, to go through the transitions of life together. In times of trouble, people find in vital congregations a network of support.

One of the most common images for congregations is the family. We develop programs and activities for "the church family." This is a powerful symbol, for it speaks to people's desire to be connected and involved with a caring community.

At the same time, congregations must recognize how dramatically the family is changing in every culture. In North America only a small percentage of the population lives in "nuclear" family units of husband, wife, and children. Many people live singly. Many live at great distance from their extended family of parents and other relatives. In vital congregations, "the church family" especially recognizes and welcomes the needs and interests of single persons and single parents.

Vital congregations know the challenges of caring community in modern culture. In societies where people place great value on privacy and individual choice, community is an object of both hunger and hesitation. People want mutual support, but are often tentative about making commitments that would make real community possible.

Congregations must find a balance between accepting

A primary concern for the future is to maintain a solid spiritual focus amid the pains of growth.
Hockessin Church
Hockessin, Delaware

We would meet for a simple meal and program in the old basement with its shiny red painted floors, pillars, and low ceilings. It was a scene of joy and sharing, where we felt a wonderful sense of "family"—warmth, caring, sharing—not only in our group, but for others many miles away.
First Church
Winfield, Kansas

As we grow it becomes harder to integrate new members.
Middletown Church
Middletown, Maryland

"Many memories about the church are part of our family history."
Kern Memorial Church
Oak Ridge, Tennessee

We sponsored a family from Poland who came here seeking political asylum. We provided a home, furnishings, food and other necessities to help them establish a new life.
Calvary Church
Latham, New York

*Help us accept each other as Christ accepted us;
teach us as sister, brother, each person to embrace.
Be present, Lord, among us, and bring us to believe
we are ourselves accepted and meant to love and live.*
Fred Kaan
The United Methodist Hymnal, No. 560
Hope Publishing Co.; 380 S. Main Pl.; Carol Stream, IL 60188.

VITAL CONGREGATIONS—FAITHFUL DISCIPLES

Our primary challenge as we face the 1990s is to maintain a sense of oneness as we grow. Most of us remember when this church was one big family. We knew each other and it was easy to care about each other. As we grow we will be challenged to maintain that care for one another.

Garber Church
New Bern, North Carolina

We open our church for community functions, musical performances, group meetings, such as pre-school. We began an AIDS education program when there were many in the community and the congregation that felt very uneasy about even mentioning the subject. Our church sponsored the Peace March when other churches would not participate and became hostile to the group. The state-wide marchers said ours was the largest gathering they had experienced. Out of the march came the Peace Choir, with some of our people participating, and then a supper in our church building for a choir from the USSR that performed here. So our "outreach" to the community takes many forms.

Coupeville Church
Coupeville, Washington

We are aware to varying degrees that we face technological changes that will make us look at our faith differently. We know that the church needs to be dealing with these issues now rather than waiting and reacting after the changes are commonplace. In particular, technological changes we face in this farming area include seed banks and genetic manipulation.

Woodbine Church
Woodbine, Kansas

that tentativeness and challenging it. Perhaps the most distinctive aspect of Christian discipleship in today's social context is that it requires and thrives on community and hospitality. To give up the effort to invite people into community is to surrender part of our life with Christ.

Vital congregations link people together in acts of caring. They prepare people for visiting in hospitals, for consoling those who grieve. Caring is not left exclusively to the professional clergy. Rather, the pastor leads the way in teaching skills of care-giving so that the laity become an essential part of this ministry.

Yet if vital congregations are bound in Christian community, they are also always practicing the openness of hospitality. Their care extends to anyone in the larger community who has a critical need. The well-being of the whole community is their concern.

Seeking Moral Discernment

The moral dilemmas facing humanity today grow more complex with each passing day. We struggle to understand the Christian witness in questions of hunger, warfare, medical technology, AIDS, abortion, the farm crisis, urban poverty, human sexuality, and many others. The multiplying of ethical dilemmas threatens to overwhelm our efforts to be faithful to the gospel.

Congregations fed by life with Christ must guide people into moral discussion. Vital congregations provide a structure for Christians to wrestle together with decisions that face us as individuals, as communities, as societies. Together we can be communities of moral discernment, in which, through informed study and disciplined prayer, we begin to see the way ahead for actions that will be signs of God's intentions for the world.

A powerful legacy of witness supports our thinking and acting on moral issues. The Social Principles of The United Methodist Church represent decades of effort to speak the Word of the gospel in rapidly changing social situations. We must continue the dialogue as we share the dilemmas and decisions of our homes, workplaces, and communities.

Raising Up New Leaders

Congregations are the basic communities of faith within which new leaders for the church must be identified, called, prepared, and supported. The raising up of committed imaginative leaders is a gift of the Holy Spirit and a sign of life in Christ. For it is Christ who calls leaders for God's mission in the world, and the Spirit who gives them the gifts of leadership.

Our congregations are at a critical point: a new generation of lay and clergy leaders must be prepared to guide the church into the next century. We need many new ministers ordained to pastoral leadership as retirements increase over the next decade. We need laity trained for missional leadership to develop local church ministries and to oversee the work of our agencies and institutions. We need missionaries, counselors, teachers, and many others skilled in the helping professions to extend the mission of the church.

The preparation of such leaders is more crucial than ever. Seminaries, pastors schools, lay institutes, and workshops must stand ready to provide both study of Christian tradition and training in the skills of leadership.

Local church congregations remain the fertile ground from which new leaders grow. Christ announces his call to discipleship to all. But our responsibility in the congregation is to make the call to leadership definite as we identify potential leaders among us, challenge them with the task, and support them as they prepare to lead the church.

Equipping the People of God for Witness in Everyday Life

The people of God who make up vital congregations are the apostles or messengers of Christ in everyday life. Yet a growing gulf exists between Sunday church life and the Monday working world. Many of us have little idea how to connect our faith with our daily activities of work, school, leisure, or civic involvement. Many of us are overwhelmed by the situations into which we are thrust by virtue of our employment: unethical business practices; drug and alcohol use in the workplace;

In its thirty years of existence, the First Church in Baguio City, The Philippines, has produced three clergy persons and two deaconesses, and provided support to an evangelization program to the many mountain tribes living close to the city.

Tradition plays a major part in our church—at least with the older members. Sometimes we worry that the younger generations will not carry forward our rich Christian heritage. Will we speak to posterity from these walls? What will our message be? Will others be compelled to follow?

Ebenezer Church
Newberry, South Carolina

During the Depression, the Wesley Foundation at the University of Illinois was saved only because some of the church's members mortgaged their own homes and donated that money.

Wesley Church
Urbana, Illinois

When lay people and clergy think about ministry there is a preoccupation with activities "inside" the church. Many attempts to focus on ministry in the world fizzle out as time and energy are spent on maintaining the organization of a congregation and its activities or its judicatory connections. These things are important, but something is wrong when no time or resources are left to deal with where we spend most of our lives—at work, in the family and in the larger community.

Robert E. Reber, Dean
Auburn Theological Seminary
New York, New York

VITAL CONGREGATIONS—FAITHFUL DISCIPLES

At First Church in Flemingsburg, Kentucky, a mentally impaired man in overalls sat in the second pew from the front and cried during the entire service. One man came down from the choir and put his arm around him. Others in the congregation later employed him.

"If there was any doubt as to whether the kitchen wall should have a door leading into the coffee room, it's too late now! Nothing seems to stop our people from doing what needs doing—not even a five-inch thick concrete block wall! As I saw that sledgehammer crash through that wall, I saw an image in my mind—an image of the church in the business of 'breaking barriers and opening doors.' Isn't this what the Food Pantry, the Clothing Closet, the Thrift Shop, the Each Elder Ministry, and the After-School Program are all about? And isn't this what Church School and Sunday Morning Worship are all about? 'For he is our peace, who has made us both one, and has broken down the dividing wall of hostility . . . (Eph. 2:14).'"

Istrouma Church
Baton Rouge, Louisiana

One of our ministries is Cross Clinic, a free weekly medical clinic for those who cannot afford insurance. The poor have Medicaid and the elderly Medicare, so this is for those with neither who are trying to make ends meet and can't afford to go to a doctor.

First Church
Mangum, Oklahoma

Knox Memorial Church in Manila, The Philippines, runs an elementary school, reaches out to youth and students, and supports the mission evangelism of the district with funds and personnel.

pollution of air, land, and water through industrial practices.

Vital congregations offer opportunities for people to think through, pray about, and act on their calling as part of the whole people of God. Through the Sunday school and small groups, they provide discussion settings in which people can share their moral dilemmas and consider what their role as a Christian should be in a given situation.

Vital congregations train and guide people for witness to their life in Jesus Christ with persons who do not know the Lord. They teach the ways of "friendship evangelism" through which people learn to relate to others in non-threatening ways and to help them discover the promises God has for them in life with Christ.

Vital congregations challenge people to give their time, energy, and talents to helping others. They organize business people to set up job training facilities. They recruit physicians and counselors to operate health clinics for the poor. They support teachers and social workers in forming classes in parenting, human sexuality, reading and writing, and other life skills.

Vital congregations do not find worship a haven from daily life, but a source of strength for everyday living. Through the patterns of worship and prayer in the gathered community—in praise, confession, obedience and service—we learn to connect the difficult decisions of our lives with the faith that undergirds us.

Joining in Ministries of Justice, Hope, and Peace

Congregations are a sign of life in Christ as they give their lives for the biblical vision of *shalom*: a world established in peace through just relationships. Vital congregations are apostles and missionaries of this vision.

Congregations everywhere find themselves planted in situations of suffering, conflict, and despair. Congregations must respond with efforts that continue Christ's ministry of healing and reconciliation.

In every region and every land, there are people who can find no place in the economic system. For them, hunger may be a daily reality. Often they are displaced from their homes and separated from their family roots. In many cases they are victims of domestic violence. They may have few job skills, and may be only partially literate if at all. Others may be well-educated but unable to find work. Marriages and families strain under such burdens; children are born to children, and problems are passed on to the next generation.

The prevalence of drug and alcohol abuse across all social classes indicates a deep restlessness and disorder in societies everywhere. When life apparently offers no hope of fulfillment, people hunger for experiences of power and confidence that drugs promise them. As addiction spreads and is passed to the next generation, accompanying problems of crime and violence follow.

Specialized agencies respond to these crises by providing many needed services. Congregations contribute to the support of these programs through apportioned giving and special efforts to raise money and goods. While this has provided crucial funds for these ministries, the effect has often been to separate congregations from the problems.

Vital congregations give their full support to these specialized programs, but the congregation itself gets involved with ministries that touch the lives of hurting people. **Discipleship in a vital congregation is hands-on,** serving lunch to the poor, supervising a night shelter for homeless families, handling a switchboard for job-hunting, answering the drug hotline phones.

Vital congregations are also concerned about the wider implications of human problems in their neighborhood. They join groups to lobby for legislation that will ease the flow of food to starving nations. They organize youth groups to meet after school or in the evening, to help the young develop a stronger self-image as children of a God who loves and has a purpose for them. They work for affordable housing in their region. They join in concern for the deteriorating condition of air, soil, and water in every land. They pray for the peace of all peoples, and urge governments to sit at the negotiating table to resolve their conflicts.

Vital congregations are compelled by their vision of God's reign of *shalom* to carry out ministries of justice,

I am becoming more and more aware that we are living in an addictive society. For me, any addictive behavior is a sin and I am constantly reminded that "the wages of sin is death but the gift of God is eternal life." At some point in the many conversations shared with persons closely related to this assignment, a common theme emerges. "Bishop," they say, "this is a spiritual problem, and it can only be solved by spiritual people with spiritual answers." A woman who is a recovering addict shared in a testimonial meeting: "I searched everywhere for help and nothing worked until I found Jesus and this church . . . Bishop, only the spirit of Jesus will solve our problems."

Bishop Felton E. May
Special Assignment
Washington, D.C.

A young teenager in our congregation was recently admitted to a facility for drug addiction. We helped raise money for her 42-day stay there. We sent a care basket with gifts for her to open each day. Her mother was brave enough and felt close enough to us all to stand before us in worship service one Sunday and tell us what had been going on in this young girl's life. She expressed appreciation to us for the love and care that had been extended to her and her family, and she asked for our help in trying to combat this problem in our community.

McCormick Church
McCormick, South Carolina

Worship is the most concrete characteristic of the church. In this sincere manner, the church is able to present itself as a praying church; able to express the fruit of the spirit in many activities for the salvation of the community. The church believes, even as a poor community of faith, it is able to reach out and serve the dying in the neighborhood. It rejoices that some of these come to join the church.

Wesley Church
New Haven, Connecticut

VITAL CONGREGATIONS—FAITHFUL DISCIPLES

We've a song to be sung to the nations,
that shall lift their hearts to the Lord,
a song that shall conquer evil
and shatter the spear and sword,
and shatter the spear and sword.

H. Ernest Nichol
The United Methodist Hymnal, No. 569

"I joined the Methodist Church at an early age, a member of a small rural congregation in southwestern Iowa. I later drifted away from regular Church involvement. Personal circumstances led me into Alanon eight years ago. That recovery program was my main 'church' connection for several years.

"I was looking for a church family that would accept me as I am. I also was looking for a fellowship that provided an opportunity for growth in my Christian faith. My fiance had made an important life decision to no longer drink, and was looking for a church that would provide the setting to strengthen his personal relationship with Christ as well as fellowship with other Christians.

"One Sunday, we passed Calvary Church as we had done many other Sundays. That Sunday, however, we parked the car and entered. The service was just starting. Immediately, I sensed I had come 'home'! The atmosphere was warm and open. The large paintings of Christ, simple stained glass windows, and the white altar gave me such a feeling of comfort. It was a very emotional experience for me as we all joined hands and sang, 'God be with you till we meet again.' The pastor and the church

hope, and peace. They act out their joy in the salvation and love of God through gestures of mercy in their communities. What difference will it make to the world if there are more Christians or more United Methodists? It will make a difference if the communities in which congregations serve are made more loving and just by the witness and action of the faithful.

Witnessing to Salvation in Christ

Vital congregations call people to repentance, to a new life so turned around from the old that it is like being born all over again (John 3:3-4). Vital congregations witness to the revolutionary good news of Jesus Christ through their worship, fellowship, mission programs, and every aspect of their ministry. In vital congregations there is no mistaking that in song and prayer, in sermon and sacrament, in classroom and at mealtime, in mission and outreach, the people are acting in the name of Jesus Christ.

The point at which many of our congregations have struggled is in reaching people outside of or alienated from the church. We have been hesitant to announce the gospel beyond the accepted Sunday morning hour.

But our witness is more critical than ever. We can no longer count on faith simply being passed down to the next generation. We must be more intentional in our evangelism, for which our Wesleyan heritage gives us a dynamic model.

John Wesley began his ministry as a sedate Anglican who did everything in good order, and always inside the church building. But the day came when he felt called to carry the gospel to the people. On Monday, April 2, 1739, he walked out into the grass outside Bristol, Bible in hand, found a rise on which to plant his feet, and began to preach. Many people heard him gladly and knew of salvation in Christ for the first time.

With what act of daring will today's United Methodists break loose from established molds and announce the good news of Christ?

John Wesley wanted to put his vision into action. The time had come to invite those who heard his preaching into small groups with a method for daily living. Such a pattern would upset routines and bring hardship. Would anyone really join him in such a discipline? But he called together a Methodist society, and one by one, desiring earnestly for salvation, the people came.

Are United Methodists today capable of the same discipline? Are we willing to risk making demands on people's time and commitment?

Vital congregations seek out and welcome new persons to find life in Christ. Led by the pastor, they train laity to visit people who might be ready to deepen their relationship with God, whether those people be occasional visitors or lifelong church members looking for a congregation in their new community. Visitors, inquirers, or people touched by the congregation's ministries are invited into friendship with members and into groups for study and prayer. They are quickly able to find a place in the open hospitality of the congregation.

Vital congregations contact with friendship and support people who seem alienated from the church or disillusioned in their faith. These people are included in the web of prayers and concerns that the congregation continually brings before God, that all may find the fulfillment of faith in Christ.

Evangelism is the work of sharing Jesus Christ with people; conversion is God's work and a gift of God's grace. Christ asks us simply to share with others where we have found the bread of life. Christ asks us to invite others to join the company of disciples along the journey of faith.

If we plant the seeds and nurture them, we trust that God will give the growth. The harvest, after all, belongs to God, and God can make our efforts bear fruit beyond anything we can ask or imagine.

Signs of Faithfulness in Discipleship

The signs of faithfulness in disciples who seek to follow Christ are salt and yeast in the vitality of the congregation. Congregations are made vital through the Christian life and action of the faithful, just as believers

members were so friendly and helped us both to feel welcome immediately.

"We joined the church the first Sunday in December. I am grateful to have the opportunity to worship and serve God as part of this congregation."
Calvary Church
Shakopee, Minnesota

We have many points of entry into our church through the many and varied programs and opportunities made available for all ages.
First Church
Fort Collins, Colorado

The people of God are the Church made visible in the world. It is they who must convince the world of the reality of the gospel or leave it unconvinced. There can be no evasion or delegation of this responsibility; the Church is either faithful as a witnessing and serving community, or it loses its vitality and its impact on an unbelieving world.
The Book of Discipline, 1988, ¶107

When one member was killed, within six hours every member of our church had been to the house to express their sympathy, offer help, and share grief. This caring extends right up to today (eight months later) in so many tangible and intangible ways.
Bowen's Creek Church
Roark, Kentucky

VITAL CONGREGATIONS—FAITHFUL DISCIPLES

O Holy God,
  open unto me
    light for my darkness,
    courage for my fear,
    hope for my despair.
O Loving God,
  open unto me
    wisdom for my confusion,
    forgiveness for my sins,
    love for my hate.
O God of peace,
  open unto me
    peace for my turmoil,
    joy for my sorrow,
    strength for my weakness.
O generous God,
  open my heart
    to receive all your gifts.
Amen.

Howard Thurman
The United Methodist Hymnal, No. 489

By permission of the Howard Thurman Educational Trust; 2020 Stockton St.; San Francisco, CA 94133. From *Meditations of the Heart.*

Some years ago, when our church family was meeting to vote on whether or not to become a reconciling congregation, having held a number of meetings in various formats already, those present were distressed to find that some people were still ready to debate the issue all over again and at the tops of their voices. In an emotionally charged atmosphere, our lay leader took the floor and said, simply, "I cannot quote chapter and verse from the Bible as some of you can. I'm no expert on homosexuality. All I know is that Jesus said, 'Love your neighbor as yourself.' He didn't say what kind of neighbor. He just said, 'Love your neighbor.' I think we should do just that." The motion passed.

Wallingford Church
Seattle, Washington

---

are built up in faith through the life of a congregation.

Faithful discipleship has in the United Methodist heritage traditionally been called holiness, or holy living. In the New Testament the "holy ones" were the "saints," in Paul's usage a term for every believer striving to live by the Spirit as a new creature in Christ (Romans 15:25; 1 Corinthians 16:1).

Discipleship is the fruit in action of a life with Christ. It is the outward and visible sign of one's seriousness in following Jesus on the road to service and even to a cross. It is a way of life to which every believer is called.

Christians have suffered much confusion about the meaning of discipleship, and United Methodists much uncertainty about the distinctiveness of our own tradition of holiness. Some Christians believe that true disciples are identified only by having a certain type of experience of Jesus Christ. Many persons have been deeply touched and had their lives changed by such personal experiences.

Yet Christ does not come to every person in the same way, and insisting on immediate signs of conversion holds Christ to the limits of just one type of experience. Moreover, the conversion or reorientation of a person's life requires a lifetime of companionship with the Lord. While a person may or may not have a single life-changing experience of Christ's presence, all people can follow Christ into places of ministry and give themselves to Christ's work.

Other Christians have looked upon discipleship as a set of moral rules for living. These rules have been considered a kind of minimum standard for salvation. Many people have found such absolutes a great comfort and guide for living. Yet relying on such regulations can lead to a return to the law even among gospel people, and the freedom of the Christian to respond to God's reconciling love with spontaneous acts of love can be reduced to a mere formality.

The rules of Christian living that arose in nineteenth century North America often were translated into public laws governing entire communities, states, or even the nation. But the whole environment for that understanding of discipleship is gone. Christians cannot count on the state to enforce certain moral practices. The cultural climate is far more pluralistic. Christians are forced to ask less how their views can become public law, and more how their own lives can model and reflect the values of Jesus.

Therefore our most basic need for the life of discipleship today is the discipline that will keep us in Christ's fellowship. A discipline is a way of life that teaches; it shapes or forms those who follow it. It does not produce people who all decide or act exactly the same way. It can, though, produce dispositions or habits of thought that give its followers a certain orientation in life.

His grasp of this was part of John Wesley's genius. He did not require of Methodist people any single experience of Jesus Christ. Nor did he lay out a set of laws by which people would be saved. He was repulsed by the idea that people would abide by commandments without the loving heart and lively spirit to go with it.

As in many things Methodist, Wesley sought a middle ground. He advocated "methods" by which people could, over a lifetime, find closer fellowship with Christ. He believed that those who followed the disciplines of Christian living would find themselves stamped with the image of Christ on their heart as they were made perfect in love. And he was convinced that the more people were committed to "holy living," the closer both church and society would move toward the kingdom of God.

The whole church has much to celebrate today in the accelerating recovery of these disciplines. Through them people everywhere are finding courage and hope for their own witness to Jesus Christ in daily life. These disciplines are themselves signs of faithful discipleship.

Participating in the Life of a Congregation

Faithful disciples are upheld in Christian living through their participation in the worship, fellowship, and mission of a local church congregation. In the congregation the sacraments are celebrated; disciples hear again their baptismal calling, and enjoy again the presence of Christ at the Communion table. The Word is read and interpreted. Prayers are offered for the needs of individuals and of the whole world. Through the cycle

The early Methodist people did something truly remarkable: they developed an intense internal community life without withdrawing from the world. They maintained jobs; carried on family life; bought and sold in the marketplace. Yet they had an intensity of community life which shaped their moral values and to a remarkable degree kept them from being squeezed into the world's mold.

This is one of those tension points where the church with time tends to slide off to one side or the other—either to become so much a part that the salt becomes tasteless, or to so withdraw from the world that the light never touches the world's darkness. A community of disciples which is both salt and light maintains a redemptive balance between separation from the world, nurtured by specific, scheduled, disciplined forms of community, and active involvement in the world of economics, politics, and social interaction.

Howard A. Snyder, Professor
United Theological Seminary
Dayton, Ohio

She is a widowed great-grandmother who, with her daughters, son, grandchildren and great grandchildren is active as a member of the church. Whenever someone accomplishes something noteworthy, she drops him or her a note. When a member is in the hospital or sick at home, she is the first to bring a tray of food. A constant visitor in homes, she is in her eighties, but is always on the "go."

First Church
Winnfield, Louisiana

VITAL CONGREGATIONS—FAITHFUL DISCIPLES

We have open communion and encourage independent thinking within certain theological limits. We do infant baptism and use United Methodist ritual in worship. We have several district officers in our congregation, and we participate frequently in district and conference activities. Our committee organization reflects our Methodist heritage, as does our frequent participation in potlucks!

Wesley Church
Vergennes, Illinois

It is therefore expected of all who continue therein that they should continue to evidence their desire of salvation.

First: By doing no harm, by avoiding evil of every kind, especially that which is most generally practiced . . .

Secondly: By doing good, by being in every kind merciful after their power; as they have opportunity, doing good of every possible sort, and, as far as possible, to all. . . .

Thirdly: By attending upon all the ordinances of God; such are:

The public worship of God.
The ministry of the Word, either read or expounded.
The Supper of the Lord.
Family and private prayer.
Searching the Scriptures.
Fasting or abstinence.

The General Rules of Our United Societies
The Book of Discipline, 1988, ¶68

Not my brother, not my sister,
but it's me, O Lord,
standing in the need of prayer.

Afro-American spiritual
The United Methodist Hymnal, No. 352

of the Christian year, from Advent and Christmas through Lent and Easter to Pentecost, disciples learn to follow the life of Christ as the pattern for all of life.

Congregations offer the fellowship and learning so vital to sustaining the Christian life over time. Here disciples can bring their questions and struggles. Here they can find support and common convictions. The mission of the congregation involves disciples in acting on the way of Christ in concrete forms; disciples learn the joy and challenge of giving themselves on behalf of others.

Searching the Scriptures

Faithful disciples find in daily readings of Scripture new insights and strengths for their walk with Christ. The stories of women and men who put their trust in God are inspiring. The circumstances of each day can make any given verse come alive with new meaning. In a video age such reading can be a hard discipline, but without it the Christian walk is aimless.

Many formats for daily Scripture reading are now available. Through a daily lectionary readers work their way gradually through entire books of the Old and New Testaments and become familiar with whole stories rather than just verses or pieces of stories. The daily reading or singing of psalms also helps people become familiar with all the psalms and their many avenues of approach to God.

Living a Life of Prayer

Faithful disciples practice regular times of prayer as part of daily living. They experience the various attitudes of prayer: praise, thanksgiving, invocation, confession, petition, intercession, benediction. They spend time in silence, asking God to enter the space created in lives too full of busy-ness and distraction.

Prayer groups are springing up all across the church, through which people experience fellowship with Christ and with one another. Finding time and quiet is more and more difficult today. But in prayer we discover a whole new freedom; we can find perspective on the demands of daily living. In groups, we discover the

OFFERING OUR RESPONSE TO THE LORD

remarkable energy and expectation that come from praying for others and being prayed for oneself. In bringing the world before God in prayer, we no longer stand hopeless before the overwhelming problems that confront humanity, but are strengthened in the hope of God's promise of salvation.

Fasting

Faithful disciples regularly fast or abstain from certain food and drink in order to remind themselves of the gifts of God that sustain life. Human appetites are endless; human beings are forever hungry creatures. Through fasting, disciples recognize those hungers and remember that it is in God's providence to give us our daily bread.

Many people in the world today have far too much to eat, while many others starve. Many United Methodists have more than enough to eat, and to spare. Fasting reminds us that God is the source of life. God loves those who hunger as well as those who are satisfied. Food is not a market product in the kingdom of God, and never to be a bargaining chip between nations. Food is simply the sustenance of life, to be shared for the well-being of all.

Fasting runs counter to a culture of consumption. We are bombarded with messages that the way to happiness lies in consuming more food, drink, and possessions. Fasting and abstinence free us to discover fulfillment in ways that do not divide us from our neighbor or do increasing damage to the earth.

Many Christians testify to the strength and insight to be gained from fasting. Cleared from the stupor of heavy eating, made aware of our own appetites, we see more clearly what God would have us do. We are given power to resist temptation and overcome evil (Matthew 17:21). We are given the courage to act so that others will see God's love in us.

Living Simply

Faithful disciples live simply. They are diligent in limiting their consumption of earth's resources. If in fasting they recall God's gifts of food, in living simply

Spirit of God, descend upon my heart;
wean it from earth; through all its pulses move;
stoop to my weakness, mighty as thou art,
and make me love thee as I ought to love.

George Croly
The United Methodist Hymnal, No. 500

The days will come when the bridegroom will be taken away from them and then they will fast in those days.

Luke 5:35

Christ be with me, Christ within me,
  Christ behind me, Christ before me,
Christ beside me, Christ to win me,
  Christ to comfort and restore me,

127

VITAL CONGREGATIONS—FAITHFUL DISCIPLES

Christ beneath me, Christ above me,
  Christ in quiet, Christ in danger,
Christ in hearts of all that love me,
  Christ in mouth of friend and stranger.
Prayer of St. Patrick

"I grew up in this church and was here when the present structure was built. The stained glass windows are important to me, because I remember the paper we had on the windows in the old church to make them look like stained glass. My parents mortgaged their home to buy the pews when this building was built."
Humphreys Memorial Church
Tornado, West Virginia

S. Trowen Nagbe Church in Sinkor, Monrovia, Liberia, provides ministries of visitation to the lonely and elderly, and offers food, clothing, and shelter to prisoners and the homeless.

they recall the joys God provides in the human relationships that sustain life's meaning.

The world market system is an endless conveyor belt of consumer items, material things that make life more comfortable but also more complicated. The gap between haves and have-nots only widens by this means. In simple living, Christians identify with those whose daily struggle is simply to live.

John Wesley worried that "wherever riches have increased, (exceeding few are the exceptions,) the essence of religion, the mind that was in Christ, has decreased in the same proportion." In fact, one of the ironic consequences of the diligence and frugality he urged on Methodist people was that they accumulated more goods. "Hence they proportionably increase in pride, anger, in the desire of the flesh, the desire of the eyes, and the pride of life."

There is little evidence in today's world that Wesley's concerns were ill-founded. Truly, simplicity of living makes faithful disciples exceptional people, and is a sign of life in Christ.

Stewarding the Gifts of Life

Faithful disciples are stewards (in Greek, *oikonomoi*, household managers) of the grace or gift given them by the Spirit (1 Peter 4:10). No area of their lives can be untouched by this stewardship, for the claim of Christ is upon them. Their stewardship extends to the *oikoumene*, the whole household of earth, for God intends to transform all creation in the fullness of time (Romans 8:22; Colossians 1:19-20).

Faithful disciples support in every way they can the carrying forward of Christ's ministry through the community of faith. Paul appealed to the early Christians to "put aside and save whatever extra you earn" to contribute to the mission of the church (1 Corinthians 16:2). Regular, proportional giving is essential to being part of the covenant community of a congregation and the larger covenant connection of the church.

We enjoy a living legacy of agencies and institutions that represent the United Methodist vision of the

Christian mission in education, health care, social welfare, and other fields. The faithful work of these institutions has touched and changed more lives than could ever be calculated.

Yet we are pressed to maintain these agencies and sometimes question why money is requested of us for administering them. We need to evaluate more carefully the ministries provided by our institutions. We need to become more aware of the exciting work that they are accomplishing. And we need to examine untapped resources and funds not being well spent in our congregations.

But if we United Methodists are to express our imagination for what God is calling us to do in the next century, and to put our vision into action through programs of witness and service that require money to support them, then each of us as faithful disciples must discover a deeper, more compelling sense of Christian stewardship of all of life.

Stewardship is a discipline of the spirit through which both individuals and congregations find life in Christ. The opportunity of helping others through our gifts brings us to life and sets us on fire with the spirit of serving Jesus Christ.

Doing Good to Others

Faithful disciples express their love of Christ by acting in his way: comforting those who grieve; praying with the sick and dying; visiting the poor, and those in prison. They make themselves instruments of God's grace by trying to be where Christ would be, as Christ's body in the world.

The actual visit to the prison, the time spent in hospital rooms, the prayers with a poor family in their home: these are the disciplines to which Christians are called. They are means of grace through which disciples discover the presence of Christ and the joy and challenge of ministry in Christ's name. Through them disciples develop an outlook on other human beings, shaped not by public stereotypes, but by a God who creates and gives purpose to every human life. Racial slurs, prejudgments of teen mothers, slogans that

Our Covenant

We, the church family of Middletown Community United Methodist Church, in response to our understanding of God's presence in our world, intend through prayer, personal awareness and hospitality to

—*Learn of the life of Christ and practice what we learn every day*

—*Live lives of gratitude, willing to face our fears as well as to speak the truth directly, in love*

—*Have the courage to change our own lives and to risk action toward growth in our community*

—*Be committed to increased consciousness of our connectedness with all life forms in our environment*

—*Be advocates for justice for all people without bias regarding race, color, beliefs or lifestyles*

—*Recognize ourselves as needy persons who are learning to be aware of our own addictions, emptiness and isolation and how to struggle together toward healing*

—*Be centered in the children; celebrating life and accepting its completion.*

Then, by the empowerment that comes through relationship to each other in God we can become a church without walls radiating the love, the hope and the joy we experience in the life of God through the Spirit.

Community Church
Middletown, California

When one member was called home to England by family illness, the Joy Center in Roark, Kentucky, spontaneously took up an offering to send her and her family. In about two hours, $700 (over $40 per family) came in—this in a congregation with forty percent unemployment.

VITAL CONGREGATIONS—FAITHFUL DISCIPLES

I am personally convinced that the mission of the church is not about Christian expansionism. When it comes to the confession of our faith in the world, we must do this through an unambiguous commitment to the world itself, motivated only by obedience to Jesus Christ, that is, by participating in his love and care for the creation, his stewardship. Our discipleship means "being there;" not just talk about Jesus but actually living the life of Jesus (of the body of Christ) in the world; being salt, yeast, light, and seed. Our mission is our stewardship of life in the kingdom of death.

But this should not translate into a reduction of the gospel to "issues." Christians are driven because they are disciples of one who loves the world, who therefore judges it, and who is seeking to mend it.

Douglas John Hall, Professor
McGill University
Montreal, Canada

Our name is Wesley Chapel. We try to be true to our tradition. As John Wesley said, "The world is my parish." We take that seriously. We are evangelical and mission-minded. We believe in world missions and support them actively. We have a concern for the hungry, not only the physically hungry but the spiritually hungry as well.

Wesley Chapel Church
New Albany, Indiana

"explain" poverty or AIDS, all fall by the wayside when Christian disciples get personally involved in the lives of people in need, even as Jesus was.

Advocating Peace and Justice

Faithful disciples already live more peacefully by living simply and doing good to others. But the massive problems of hunger and habitation that face humanity today require the involvement of denominations, aid organizations, governments, and business corporations. Faithful disciples are tireless in doing what they can for improving world food distribution, reducing the waste of resources on military armaments, and encouraging negotiation for resolving conflicts.

There are many avenues for expressing this discipleship: through political elections and legislative processes; through gifts of time and money to efforts such as Volunteers in Mission; through development of programs in business corporations or universities that will coordinate resources for responding to human problems.

The churches have often been the strongest, sometimes the only, advocates for people who have nothing, and whom the political systems overlook. Today United Methodists must claim that role as never before.

Sharing the Faith

Disciples become faith-full, filled with faith, as they live by the disciplines of holiness that bring them into fellowship with Christ. Holding fast to Christ Jesus, disciples experience forgiveness of their sins, healing of their brokenness, and strengthening of their ministry in Christ's name. They are not delivered from hardships or tests of faith; but they trust that in the power of Christ they are journeying toward that city where God is all in all (Revelation 22:5).

Faithful disciples cannot help but share their faith with others, and invite them to join in the journey of God's covenant people. Touched by Christ's healing and forgiveness, disciples pray for Christ's presence with others. Challenged and invigorated by Christ's calling to follow, disciples urge others to join in the Christian way.

Such sharing of the faith is the deepest form of

friendship. It expresses a genuine and lasting care for other persons. It opens the way to a lifelong fellowship along a pilgrimage that leads to the everlasting city where we will be sojourners and wayfarers no more (Hebrews 13:14).

Together we hope in what is not yet seen, and await it with patience (Romans 8:25). We trust that God's intentions for us and for all creation will come to fruition in the fullness of time. For our hope is not for this life only, but looks to a world yet to come (1 Corinthians 15:19).

Giving God the Glory

Faithful disciples live their whole lives to the glory of God. In their disciplines they are making choices that point to a God whose love, mercy, justice, and hope were revealed most clearly in Jesus Christ. Christ is no longer with us in the flesh (2 Corinthians 5:16); now it is the work of faithful disciples to point to that same eternal God.

Contemporary life offers many options that give no glory to God. Massive piles of garbage, acres of wrecked automobiles, pools of foamy slime on beaches, remains of animals slaughtered for their skins or tusks, all give mute testimony to the greed and carelessness that stalks human life globally. Our days on earth can be spent out of time and out of mind in a whirl of consumption, noise, and distraction, in which everything is shut out but individual experience.

Christians give God the glory, which must always mean standing over against this mindlessness with the mind that was in Christ. For Jesus took the form of a servant, even to the point of giving his life, so that we might live. Christian servanthood requires attention—paying attention, listening to Christ's words for today, attending to the cries of need around us—and it requires intention—choosing to give ourselves for others.

Neither is easy in today's cultures. What is distinctive about faithful disciples is their attention to following Christ, and their intention to go with him even against the current. For Christ and Christ alone is the living water that wells up to eternity.

Mission to us is evangelism grown tangible and comprehensive: comprehensive in that it cares for every aspect of human need and comprehensive in that it reaches into all the world. The world starts at our door step.

First Church
Mt. Pleasant, Iowa

We write in defense of creation. We do so because the creation itself is under attack. Air and water, trees and fruits and flowers, birds and fish and cattle, all children and youth, women and men live under the darkening shadows of a threatening nuclear winter. We call The United Methodist Church to more faithful witness and action in the face of this worsening nuclear crisis. It is a crisis that threatens to assault not only the whole human family but planet earth itself, even while the arms race itself cruelly destroys millions of lives in conventional wars, repressive violence, and massive poverty.

The Council of Bishops
Pastoral Letter,
In Defense of Creation

To God be the glory,
to God be the glory,
to God be the glory
for the things he has done.
With his blood he has saved me;
with his power he has raised me;
to God be the glory
for the things he has done.

Andrae Crouch
The United Methodist Hymnal, No. 99

Copyright 1971, Communiqué Music (Administered by Copyright Management, Inc.)

By consequence, whatsoever [a Methodist] doeth, it is all to the glory of God.

John Wesley

HOLY COMMUNION: SIGN OF RECONCILIATION AND LOVE

Having offered ourselves to God, we come now to the Lord's Table. We come to ask the blessings of forgiveness and acceptance as disciples of the Lord. We come to seek food for the journey. We come to bind our commitment with one another and with the Lord to be faithful witnesses and servants of the Kingdom.

We bring gifts of bread and wine as signs of all that God has done for us in Jesus Christ. When we break the bread, we have a share in the body of Christ broken on the cross that we might be made whole. In the passing of the cup, we have a share in the blood of Christ poured out for us and for our redemption.

When we eat and drink at the Lord's Table, we know that Jesus Christ is with us. Our eyes are opened to the presence of Christ, and we know ourselves received and reconciled with God and with one another. Our eyes are opened to the vision of following Christ, and we are fed and strengthened for the journey of discipleship.

Given newness of life and freshness of sight at the Table, we rise to be ourselves signs of God's reconciling love. Sealed by the sign of the new covenant in Christ's blood, we rise to make our congregations signs of the new community that is in Christ.

VITAL CONGREGATIONS—FAITHFUL DISCIPLES

For the bread which you have broken,
for the wine which you have poured,
for the words which you have spoken,
now we give our thanks, O Lord.

Louis F. Benson
The United Methodist Hymnal, No. 614

"*As a child growing up in our old church, I remember the cross which had lights imbedded on it. On First Sunday Communion at night, all the lights would be turned off and only the lighted cross and Sanctuary lights would be on. The cross in our new church is plain, but it brings back memories of a warm, glorious moment in my life when the warmth and glory of God were shown as members bowed in reverence to take the Lord's Supper.*"

Saint Mark Church
Baton Rouge, Louisiana

Guide me, O thou great Jehovah,
pilgrim through this barren land.
I am weak, but thou art mighty;
hold me with thy powerful hand.
Bread of heaven, bread of heaven,
feed me till I want no more.

William Williams
The United Methodist Hymnal, No. 127

Because there is one bread, we who are many are one body, for we all partake of the one bread. (1 Corinthians 10:17)

At the Table of the Lord's Supper, Christian congregations find their center in the living presence of Jesus Christ. As disciples faithfully seeking their Lord gather around to share in this Holy Communion, they are made "one with Christ, one with each other, and one in ministry to all the world."

In celebrating together this Eucharist, which means "thanksgiving," the people of God remember with thankfulness God's mighty acts in the life, death, and resurrection of Jesus Christ. In the Eucharist the people of God proclaim the mystery of hope and promise: "Christ has died; Christ is risen; Christ will come again" (from A Service of Word and Table I, *The United Methodist Hymnal,* page 10).

Jesus himself gave the disciples these signs. Breaking the bread at his last supper with them, he gave thanks, and said to them, "This is my body, which is given for you. Do this in remembrance of me." Then he took the cup, gave thanks, and passing it to them, said, "This cup that is poured out for you is the new covenant in my blood" (Luke 22:19-20).

In repeating these same signs, congregations are united with Christ anew. The bread and cup are placed on the Table as the gifts of the people, an offering of thanksgiving for the forgiveness and reconciliation that is ours in Christ.

Yet the bread made of earth's grains and the fruit of the vine are first of all God's gifts to us. They recall the manna in the wilderness by which God fed the people Israel: a bread that could not be stored or hoarded, but could only be received and shared as a gift to sustain them for the journey (Exodus 16:4-5, 14-18). At the Table we receive again the bread of heaven, this time as a taste of eternity. Jesus said, "Whoever eats of this bread will live forever; and the bread that I will give for the life of the world is my flesh" (John 6:51).

So in bringing gifts to the Table, the people of God are only doing what God has already done in giving us the

HOLY COMMUNION: SIGN OF RECONCILIATION AND LOVE

bread of life. The act of giving is itself a sacred act. In giving themselves for others, faithful disciples become an outward and visible sign of the grace of the Lord Jesus Christ redeeming the world.

When the people eat the bread and drink the cup, they share in the body and blood of Christ. Through Christ's sacrifice on the cross, God offers to all who earnestly repent of their sins a place at the table of redemption. In eating this food, disciples become "partakers in the divine nature" and rise to "newness of life" in Jesus Christ (from A Service of Word and Table IV, *The United Methodist Hymnal*, pages 29-30). By this meal the people of God become Christ's body alive and active in the world.

Nowhere is the universality of God's love in Christ Jesus, or the unity-in-diversity of those who seek Christ, more apparent than at the Lord's Table. United Methodism celebrates open Communion. All who worship in the congregation and genuinely desire a life with Christ are welcome to commune. They need not be church members, adults, or even baptized Christians. Children may receive the elements, as may any person of any (or no) religious background who comes to the Table seeking the grace of Jesus Christ. For at the Table all who desire the means of grace have a place; and the Lord has promised to meet us there.

So the people come, in all their remarkable diversity: young and old, of varied colors of skin, receiving the bread in hands smooth with youth or gnarled with years of labor, some convinced of the power of Jesus Christ in their lives, some trying to find out who Jesus is. And by the miracle of his presence, Jesus Christ transforms them into a congregation who together can serve in his name.

Here indeed is a foretaste of the heavenly banquet in which everyone is invited to the Table: "the poor, the crippled, the blind, and the lame," people from every crossroad of life (Luke 14:16-24). In the Kingdom everyone has enough to eat and to spare, and everyone enjoys fellowship with the Lord.

Holy Communion is the center of congregational life. Through it the people become a congregation, united in

Examine yourselves, and only then eat of the bread and drink of the cup. For all who eat and drink without discerning the body, eat and drink judgment against themselves.
1 Corinthians 11:28-29

But experience shows the gross falsehood of that assertion, that the Lord's Supper is not a converting ordinance. Ye are the witnesses. For many now present know, the very beginning of your conversion to God (perhaps, in some, the first deep conviction) was wrought at the Lord's Supper.
John Wesley

I joined the church during the city's racial strife, looking for a nonsegregated church where everybody's background was affirmed, and I found it here. We have twenty different nationalities represented, and we are united!
Church of All Nations
Boston, Massachusetts

Members of St. Paul Church in Clarksdale, Mississippi, gather for church dinners—for fun, fellowship, and food. And they take turns in the soup kitchen serving anyone who is hungry. Ministry for this congregation is feeding people.

All kinds of injustice, racism, separation and lack of freedom are radically challenged when we share in the body and blood of Christ. Through the eucharist the all-renewing grace of God penetrates and restores human personality and dignity. The eucharist involves the believer in the central event of the world's history.

VITAL CONGREGATIONS—FAITHFUL DISCIPLES

As participants in the eucharist, therefore, we prove inconsistent if we are not actively participating in this ongoing restoration of the world's situation and the human condition.

Baptism, Eucharist, and Ministry
Faith and Order Commission
World Council of Churches

"The first service we attended was an evening dedication-communion service. Our fourteen-month-old granddaughter accompanied us to communion; everyone welcomed us like family. All three of us still attend and take communion together every first Sunday."

Pleasant Hill Church
Olive Branch, Mississippi

North Hialeah Church, Hispanic, in Hialeah, Florida, celebrates the "Agape" feast every year. This celebration involves every department of the church and takes a lot of work and time, but is central to the congregation's life together.

One time during a service, the chancel curtain fell on the pastor as he moved to serve communion. It took us a while to regain composure. This is a place to laugh.

St. Paul's Church
Lawton, Michigan

"The communion rail is a place of personal commitment and closeness to God. I remember the times that I have felt touched by God at the altar."

Petal Church
Petal, Mississippi

one body as the body of Christ in the world, fed as one people in order to offer the bread of life to the world. This sacrament has been too little celebrated in The United Methodist Church. The time has come for it to hold its central place as a source of vitality for congregations.

John Wesley declared regular attendance upon the sacraments to be a basic discipline of holiness. He deliberately arranged Methodist meetings so as not to conflict with the Anglican services where Communion was available. The Methodists in North America, however, had few ordained clergy to administer the sacrament. After breaking with the Church of England, they could rarely offer Communion to the people.

On the frontier the Methodists worshiped through hymn-singing, prayer, and preaching. Traditions such as regular "love feasts" of sharing the bread and cup were widely practiced throughout the nineteenth century. Primarily the Evangelical United Brethren and some annual conferences, especially in the former black Central Jurisdiction, kept this practice alive. Many black congregations have retained a central place for Holy Communion through the tradition of the "first Sunday," on which worship is made even more celebrative in an atmosphere of solemn joy.

Such was not the situation in many predominantly Anglo congregations. Soon it was common to hear United Methodist people say that Communion just took too long, or was too "high church," or was so special that it should be reserved for only three or four Sundays a year.

Today those attitudes are changing rapidly. People everywhere are realizing the beauty and joy of Communion. People are discovering ways to make the celebration of the Eucharist the most anticipated event in a congregation's worship life. The services approved for use in United Methodist churches express varying moods and interpretations of the sacrament, even as they provide for more singing and other congregational participation in the ritual itself.

A heightened awareness of the sacrament of Holy Communion can transform the whole sacramental sense of a congregation. It sharpens the senses of the people

HOLY COMMUNION: SIGN OF RECONCILIATION AND LOVE

for seeing and naming those holy moments when God's grace is broken for the world. For grace comes not just in bread at the Table, but in human touches of love and service. The disciples' eyes were opened to Christ when he met them on the road to Emmaus and came into the house to break bread with them (Luke 24:30-31). So now faithful disciples who partake of the Lord's Supper find their eyes opened to the Christ in the faces of human needs, longings, and hopes.

The sacraments at the center of congregational life carry with them yet a further claim: that congregations are themselves signs of the living God as they gather for worship and scatter to serve. In every act of ministry, congregations give witness to the love of Christ that is transforming the world. In using their own gifts in service to the Lord, they point beyond themselves to the one Holy Spirit who gives the gifts and who even now gives the power of healing and hope to those who earnestly seek it.

People today are hungry for ways to gather, to be together, to join in mutual work together. As traditional social networks of family, tribe, clan, and ethnic group dissolve in the currents of urbanization and mobility, people long for meaning that can come only through gathering together. They hunger for companionship, literally, breaking bread together, sharing food in the hospitality of the table.

Fellowship dinners and potluck suppers are a favorite with congregations. United Methodist people love to eat. Always the act of eating together points to the source of our fellowship, though, at the Lord's Table where we break bread in Christ's presence.

And the Table of the Lord compels us into yet more bread-breaking with the poor and hungry. Accompanying the hungry in soup kitchens and food banks, refugee shelters and bread lines, Christians find in their midst Jesus Christ, the bread of life.

At the Communion table, congregations celebrate the sign that identifies us as people of God in the discipleship of Christ. We rise from the Table blessed with the power and presence of Christ. As forgiven and reconciled people, we are sent into the world in the

You satisfy the hungry heart
with gift of finest wheat.
Come, give to us, O saving Lord,
the bread of life to eat.

Omer Westendorf
The United Methodist Hymnal, No. 629

© Copyright permission obtained, Archdiocese of Philadelphia, 1977. All rights reserved.

The first service that we had after the remodeling was almost finished was on Christmas Eve. The sanctuary wasn't quite finished, but people brought their lawn chairs, blankets and we used crates for the altar. It just didn't seem to matter how much improvising we had done, we all just enjoyed fellowshipping and worshipping on Christmas Eve together in a high spirit of love and caring for each other.

Orchards Church
Vancouver, Washington

All our meals and all our living
make as sacraments of thee,
that by caring, helping, giving,
we may true disciples be.
Alleluia! Alleluia!
We will serve thee faithfully.

Percy Dearmer
The United Methodist Hymnal, No. 632

"Draw Us Together in the Spirit's Tether" (stanza 3) by Percy Dearmer (1867-1936) © 1931, from *Enlarged Songs of Praise* reprinted by permission of Oxford University Press.

"I remember sitting here in the sanctuary and smelling the food being prepared in the Fellowship Hall for a church dinner and feeling excited that I would have a chance to see everyone after the service."

Fairmont Church
Fairmont, Minnesota

VITAL CONGREGATIONS—FAITHFUL DISCIPLES

At the monthly communion worship service at Mount Zion Church in New Orleans, Louisiana, people are there in large numbers, singing, praying, listening, witnessing, and praising God. Present are babies, children, youth, young adults, adults, senior citizens, special needs individuals, and others. People are keenly aware of the presence of the Lord. After the recessional and the extinguishing of the candles by the acolytes, members depart to serve.

Too soon we rise;
the symbols disappear;
the feast, though not the love,
is past and gone.
The bread and wine remove;
but thou art here,
nearer than ever,
still my shield and sun.

Horatius Bonar
The United Methodist Hymnal, No. 623

At one heavily attended Christmas Eve communion service at Wrightsville Church in Wrightsville Beach, North Carolina, the pastor's fifteen-month-old daughter clung to the legs of her mother (the pastor) during the distribution of the elements, tenderly reminding some in the congregation of the Nativity.

A participant noted, "Our communion rail is so broad, the entire width of the sanctuary; it reminds me of the broadness of God's love."

strength of the Spirit, "to give ourselves for others, in the name of Jesus Christ" (from A Service of Word and Table I, *The United Methodist Hymnal,* page 11).

If the bread and cup are signs of Christ's love and reconciliation, when we rise to go again into the paths of everyday life, the time is at hand for us to ask: What kind of sign are we? Are we a sign to the world that God's reign is at hand here and now? Are we a sign of the heavenly banquet of divine hospitality to which all are invited? Are we a sign of the eternal love and mercy of God who is our salvation?

The world is hungry for a sign of a God who forgives, heals, guides, and promises eternal hope. Are we such a sign? What messages do we send about who God is? Everything a congregation does sends out a message: visits to the sick, acts of service, signs on the doors (or lack thereof), orders of worship, agendas for meetings, newsletters mailed, phone calls made, money distributed. In everything, a congregation is giving a sign of who God is and what the faithful expect and hope from God. What kind of sign are we?

The United Methodist Church corporately is also a sign of who we believe God is and how we think Christ's body should act in the world. What kind of sign are we as a tradition within the church universal? The time has come to ask hard questions of ourselves in the light of Christ's sign of reconciliation that we remember at the Lord's Table.

United Methodism is at a turning point in its long journey from being an evangelical renewal movement within the established church, to becoming itself a church. At this juncture we must claim our unique heritage, preserving and reconciling the evangelical and the catholic streams that flow together from our past. We have been deeply shaped by both the campmeetings of the North American frontier and the Book of Common Prayer of the Church of England. We fit our hymns of spiritual revival into the traditional seasons of the Christian year. We hold in unity the evangelical emphasis on personal piety and the church's role as catalyst for love and justice in society.

To these creative tensions of faith and practice are

HOLY COMMUNION: SIGN OF RECONCILIATION AND LOVE

added the multiple ethnic and cultural heritages that meet in United Methodism. The many languages, customs, and understandings of faith that come from our diverse heritages are a great gift to us. They also require a continual reshaping of our connectional covenant, a task for which we need imagination and commitment. Through sharing together at the Lord's Table of the new covenant, we may be granted the reconciliation and love, the wisdom and clarity we need to become a new people in covenant together.

The place where our imagination is fed, where our vision of God's reign is brightened and our gifts for witnessing to that reign are nourished, is in Communion with our Lord. When the bread is broken, our eyes are opened, and we may discern where Christ would have us go. When the cup is shared, we know that Christ is with us, and will give us the vitality we need to serve in the name of the Lord.

We rise from the table fed for the journey of discipleship. We are ready to go out as the body of Christ, to be broken for the sake of those who suffer. We are ready to go out in the footsteps of our Lord, our life as the body of Christ poured out for the redemption and salvation of the world.

The eucharist is precious food for missionaries, bread and wine for pilgrims on their apostolic journey.

Baptism, Eucharist, and Ministry
Faith and Order Commission
World Council of Churches

I am no longer my own, but thine.
Put me to what thou wilt, rank me with whom thou wilt.
Put me to doing, put me to suffering.
Let me be employed by thee or laid aside for thee,
exalted for thee or brought low by thee.
Let me be full, let me be empty.
Let me have all things, let me have nothing.
I freely and heartily yield all things
to thy pleasure and disposal.
And now, O glorious and blessed God,
Father, Son, and Holy Spirit,
thou art mine, and I am thine. So be it.
And the covenant which I have made on earth,
let it be ratified in heaven. Amen.

A Covenant Prayer in the Wesleyan Tradition
The United Methodist Hymnal, No. 607

THE PEOPLE OF GOD ARE BLESSED AND SENT

We gather as congregations to give praise to God and to build each other up as people of faith. We give thanks for all that God has done for us. We confess ourselves before God and hear God's forgiveness announced. We listen to the Word, and respond with the gift of ourselves. We celebrate Christ's presence and power with us.

We gather only to be sent out again. Our ministry as the people of God is in the world. Christ has commissioned us to go into all the world, making disciples. Christ has promised to be with us in this task to the end of the age.

We are commissioned, we are sent. We are ambassadors for Christ in a world that longs for living water. We are signs and advocates of a vision of God's new creation. We are sent to put that vision into action.

We go prepared and strengthened by our life together in congregations, upholding one another in prayer. We go asking God's blessings, that where our wisdom and courage fail, God will supply what we need. We go in the strength and spirit of God's steadfast love.

VITAL CONGREGATIONS—FAITHFUL DISCIPLES

*God of grace and God of glory,
on thy people pour thy power;
crown thine ancient church's story;
bring her bud to glorious flower.
Grant us wisdom, grant us courage,
for the facing of this hour.*

Harry Emerson Fosdick
The United Methodist Hymnal, No. 577

Elinor Fosdick Downs; 63 Atlantic Ave.; Boston, MA 02110. Used by permission.

Nourish us in the warmth of your womb, O God. Shelter us for a little while in this time of new beginnings. How fragile we sometimes feel; how precious is new life. Hold us close, and tenderly, until we are ready to fly. Let us know the strengthening comfort of your presence.

We hear Your call to bear witness to the Good News, to the light of life in Jesus Christ. May we be co-creators with you and with each other as we join in the sharing of Your love for all people, for this earth, and even for ourselves. Help us to know mercy, to feel forgiveness, to offer justice, and to walk humbly in the way of spiritual renewal along this life's journey.

Snyder Memorial Church
Jacksonville, Florida

Last winter, on a Sunday when the ground was covered with ice and the temperature near zero, we held worship service in the fellowship hall. Each family came thinking they would be the only ones there. But the fellowship hall was filled to overflowing. A choir was formed from those present; people shared special concerns. The service was very special. Many left the service to go check on the elderly who might need help in the severe weather.

First Church
Cisco, Texas

After this the Lord appointed seventy others and sent them on ahead of him in pairs to every town and place where he himself intended to go. (Luke 10:1)

And Jesus came and said to them, "All authority in heaven and on earth has been given to me. Go therefore and make disciples of all nations, baptizing them in the name of the Father and of the Son and of the Holy Spirit, and teaching them to obey everything that I have commanded you. And remember, I am with you always, to the end of the age." (Matthew 28:18-20)

At the call of Jesus Christ, we gather as people of God to worship the Lord. In every language and in diverse forms of song and prayer, we lift our voices in praise. Born of water and the Spirit, we assemble to be refreshed in our life with Christ, and to be built up into one Body united in love and gifted for service.

We gather only to be sent out again. For by water and the Spirit we are made into ambassadors for Christ, ones whose everyday lives give witness to God's eternal salvation.

The attitudes of worship—thanksgiving, confessing, hearing, responding—create in us the basic attitudes and dispositions that govern our whole lives.

We do not sing of God's glory merely on Sunday. We speak of it every day as we see the beauty and love of God in all aspects of life.

We do not pay attention only to preaching on Sunday. We listen for God's Word of mercy and judgment in the events of daily life.

We do not bow in prayer only on Sunday. We humble ourselves in the disciplines of spiritual growth every day.

The gathered moments of the congregation are precious indeed. In a world of frantic busy-ness and distraction, of persecution and despair, we do not always find it easy or sometimes even safe to assemble for the worship and fellowship of the faithful. That there are congregations at all in this hectic world is one of God's wondrous miracles.

THE PEOPLE OF GOD ARE BLESSED AND SENT

Yet we Christians do gather. We form congregations that stay together over time. We build up caring communities in which people are supported through every circumstance of life. With a shared sense of purpose we reach out in ministry.

Bells are ringing, instruments are sounding. Footsteps are heard on the paths of the world. Our footsteps carry us into the assembly of the faithful. For a while we turn our hearts to worship God who through Jesus Christ is making all things new. We live for a time in the sanctuary of God's new creation, and our hope is restored.

The vital congregations in which Christians gather "are like trees / planted by streams of water, / which yield their fruit in its season, / and their leaves do not wither" (Psalm 1:3). For in the company of all the saints, disciples of Christ are nourished and strengthened in faithfulness. We are challenged to fulfill our calling to the ministry that Jesus has entrusted to us.

But the stream by which our congregations are planted does not stand still. It flows on toward the river, the river of the city of God. We are fed and sustained in the congregation. But our calling does not stop there.

If we wish to follow Jesus, we must always be ready to move on, to reach out, to set our feet on the highway. This is not our city. What we dream of, the vision that stirs us, is the city of our God. And toward that city we direct every word and deed and hope.

We have much for which to be thankful in United Methodism. Our church can marshal amazing resources and is funded by deep reservoirs of loyalty and zealous commitment. In every place we can claim and celebrate signs of vital congregational life and faithful discipleship.

The good news is that where we have sinned and fallen short, if only we repent and turn again to Jesus Christ, God forgives us and claims us again as God's people. We are empowered to live in the freedom of obedience to our Master.

Now the time has come—to risk, to pray, to dream, to act—as a sign of the reign of God to which Jesus points us.

Id, amigos, por el mundo,
anunciando el amor,
mensajeros de la vida,
de la paz y el perdón.

Sed, amigos, mis testigos
de mi resurrección,
Id llevando mi presencia;
con vosotros estoy.

Go, my friends, go to the world,
proclaiming love to all,
messengers of my forgiving peace,
eternal love.

Be, my friends, a loyal witness,
from the dead I arose;
"Lo, I'll be with you forever,
till the end of the world."

Cesareo Gabaraín,
trans. by Raquel Gutiérrez-Achon
and Skinner Chávez-Melo
The United Methodist Hymnal, No. 583

© 1979, Cesareo Gabaraín. Published by OCP Publications, 5536 NE Hassalo, Portland, OR 97213. All rights reserved. Used with permission.

Numbers 13 and 14 tells of twelve spies sent into the promised land. Ten came back and said to stay away. This is the bad news. But two, Joshua and Caleb, looked upon it as a challenge and said it was great.

Our congregation parallels the two, not the ten. We see good in everyone and nothing is too great a challenge.

Randolph Memorial Church
Kansas City, Missouri

VITAL CONGREGATIONS—FAITHFUL DISCIPLES

In Massinga, Mozambique, no one goes outside the protection of the village between 5 P.M. and 9 A.M., because, during the night, the army places land mines to keep away the enemy.

There is nothing "normal" in the daily life of the United Methodist pastors, but they are faithful to their calling—even to death, for the enemy bullets do not choose their victims.

Thank you for our church family and friends. We also thank you for peace, patience, and understanding. Help us to be more loving and kind. Help us to be able to say, "Here we are O Lord, send us." We pray for your acceptance of these words as we work to glorify your name through your Son, Jesus. Amen.
Griffin Church
Starkville, Mississippi

We are afflicted in every way, but not crushed; perplexed, but not driven to despair; persecuted, but not forsaken; struck down, but not destroyed; always carrying in the body the death of Jesus, so that the life of Jesus may also be made visible in our bodies. For while we live, we are always being given up to death for Jesus' sake, so that the life of Jesus may be made visible in our mortal flesh. So death is at work in us, but life in you.
2 Corinthians 4:8-12

Christ needs the church,
to live and tell his story,
to praise his love and marvel at his trust,
till, bathed in light,
awakened from the dust,
we walk with God, alive in grace and glory.
Brian Wren
The United Methodist Hymnal, No. 590
_{Hope Publishing Co.; 380 S. Main Pl.; Carol Stream, IL 60188}

The world has lost its way. Societies in search of lasting values turn to religious traditions for help. People who lack the basics of food, shelter, clothing, and work are looking desperately for sisters and brothers who care. Those who suffer the modern blights of war, famine, drugs, and racial oppression cry out for people who will stand by them in their suffering as advocates of a more just and peaceful world.

Human beings long for a word of salvation and hope. They seek the assurance that life holds ultimate meaning. Never have communities of faithful disciples witnessing to the creating, delivering, and sustaining God been more needed.

We tremble before the tasks that await us. "Whom shall I send? our Maker cries; [and] many shrink from such a choice." That God would think us worthy or capable of responding to overwhelming human problems is impossible to grasp and frightful to consider. Our little congregation? With our level of training? Given all of our own problems?

"And yet, believing God who calls knows what we are and still may be, our past defeats, our future falls, we dare to answer: Lord, send me!" (*The United Methodist Hymnal*, No. 582. Words by Fred Pratt Green. © Hope Publishing Co.: 380 S. Main Pl., Carol Stream, IL 60188).

The roof leaks, the sidewalk is sinking, the windows are cracked: *but God still calls us to be ambassadors of the love of Christ.*

The meetings drone on, nobody will volunteer to visit the hospital, less than half the committee members show up: *but God still calls us to minister in Christ's name.*

The worship is dull, the choir sings off key, the organ wheezes: *but God still calls us to lives of praise and hope.*

The membership rolls are shrinking, the pledges are falling, the nominating committee is running out of names: *but God still calls us to serve the kingdom.*

"Therefore, since it is by God's mercy that we are engaged in this ministry, we do not lose heart" (2 Corinthians 4:1). We go out in courage. We may be afflicted and perplexed, but we bear within us the resurrection life of Christ.

THE PEOPLE OF GOD ARE BLESSED AND SENT

Our identity as new creatures in Christ makes us marginal people in the eyes of the world. We go out not as those seeking recognition or acclaim, but as leaven and salt, as catalysts of hope in a hurting world.

Bells are ringing, instruments are sounding. Footsteps are heard on the paths of the world. The time has come for the church—faithful disciples nurtured, sustained, and commissioned in vital congregations—to go into the world and proclaim the gospel.

Our footsteps carry us wherever the Spirit leads us to witness to Jesus Christ.

Our footsteps carry us to the door of new neighbors, to welcome them to our community and invite them to our congregation.

Our footsteps carry us to the chair in the corner by the window, to read the Bible and pray for others.

Our footsteps carry us to the AIDS hospice, to cook a meal and share a time of reflection and devotions.

Our footsteps carry us down the sidewalks and roads, to sing Christmas carols, to process with Pentecost banners, to march in protest of the drug traffic, to hand out fliers welcoming people to the worship and mission of our church.

Our footsteps carry us to the desk, to write letters to political leaders asking them to seek peaceful resolutions of conflict between nations and peoples.

Our footsteps carry us to the office, to take time to listen to an unhappy co-worker.

Our footsteps carry us to the church planning retreat, to seek God's vision for our congregation, and to change our agenda accordingly.

Our footsteps carry us to school, to invite the student of another race to sit at our table for lunch.

Our footsteps carry us to a storefront, to prepare food for the soup kitchen and visit with the homeless.

Our footsteps carry us to the office of our congressional representative, to report foreclosures on local farms and request an increase in loans for family farmers.

Our footsteps carry us to the post office, to mail a brochure to the whole community announcing our church's mission program and inviting people to join us in the ministry of Christ's love.

Lead on, O King eternal,
till sin's fierce war shall cease;
and holiness shall whisper
the sweet amen of peace.
For not with swords loud clashing,
nor roll of stirring drums;
with deeds of love and mercy
the heavenly kingdom comes.

Ernest W. Shurtleff
The United Methodist Hymnal, No. 580

Here I am, Lord. Is it I, Lord?
I have heard you calling in the night.
I will go, Lord, if you lead me.
I will hold your people in my heart.

Dan Schutte
The United Methodist Hymnal, No. 593

Copyright © 1981 by Daniel L. Schutte and NALR, 10802 N. 23rd Ave., Phoenix, AZ 85029. All rights reserved. Used with permission. From the collection *Lord of Light* by the St. Louis Jesuits.

Oo nay thla nv hee, oo way jee nee gah dee,
  Ay dee gay you he nah quo dee dah lay hv,
Woo low sv ee dah ee say stee dee gah dah,
  Ne yv say stee no de gah dah gay you hee.

Gah lah low . . .
You woe do . . .
Nah nee way . . .
Yee hoe wah . . .
Jew jee lee . . .
An skah nee . . .
Ney ha nah . . .
Joe—sv yee . . .

Oo guh wee you hee, oo jay lee day dee gah,
  Nah wah dee say stee, ah nee eh low geh suh.
Sah quo no new stee, dee say stee je sah gah,
  Low nay, dv nah skee, day gah tee, nee say stee.

145

VITAL CONGREGATIONS—FAITHFUL DISCIPLES

Jesus, son of God—we all love Him.
  Let us all go in his footsteps,
Let us all go together in love.
  Let us all look to the Word
while we are here on earth.
Let the Savior lead us.

"Heaven Beautiful"
Cherokee Hymns, No. 36

We televise our worship service. One who objected in the beginning dropped her objections when she visited her home-bound uncle and saw his eyes light up as he talked about the service last Sunday.

First Church
Springtown, Texas

Renew your church, Lord,
your people in this land.
Save us from cheap words
and self-deception in your service.

In the power of your Spirit
transform us,
and shape us
by your cross. Amen.

John de Gruchy
The United Methodist Hymnal, No. 574

Our footsteps carry us to the county jail, to lead songs and Bible readings and prayers for the prisoners.

Our footsteps carry us to an Emmaus weekend, covenant discipleship group, or Disciple Bible study, to experience a fresh encounter with the Holy Spirit.

Our footsteps carry us to the personnel director, to urge the company to hire the unemployed woman who has been living with her children in our church's emergency shelter.

Our footsteps carry us to the public housing project, to talk with a group of young mothers about caring for infant children.

Our footsteps carry us to the television station, to deliver a videotape of our congregation's worship service and Bible study, so that people confined to home or not involved in a church can worship with us.

Our footsteps carry us to confirmation class, to share our growing faith with people who are just beginning the journey of discipleship.

Our footsteps carry us to the city council meeting, to plead for a zoning change for a half-way house on our church's street.

Our footsteps carry us to the hospital, to visit a sick friend, and look in on a stranger whose illness stranded her far from home.

Our footsteps carry us to a new neighborhood or population area, to invite people to gather in a new congregation.

Our footsteps carry us home, to tell our children the stories and to teach them the songs of our biblical faith.

Our footsteps carry us to a meeting of the annual charge conference, to acknowledge and then lay aside the statistical reports, so that we can give thanks, confess, listen for God's leading, and commit ourselves in new ways to the life and mission of our congregation.

Our footsteps carry us to the community center, to share our joy and faith in Christ with teenagers plagued by thoughts of suicide, by invitations to do drugs, by freedom for sexual experimentation.

Our footsteps carry us to the factory, to persuade a co-worker to get counseling for her alcohol problem.

Our footsteps carry us to the bank, to obtain a loan for

THE PEOPLE OF GOD ARE BLESSED AND SENT

construction of low-income housing in our church's neighborhood.

Our footsteps carry us to the high school, to challenge young people to volunteer as tutors for students who are struggling in school.

Our footsteps carry us to the kitchen of a newly divorced friend, to assure him of God's love, forgiveness, and consolation.

Our footsteps carry us to the altar, to renew our baptism, to receive the bread and cup, and thus refreshed and strengthened, to walk out into the world as disciples of the living Lord.

We go as those sent to be apostles of the good news, to make disciples, to share our faith and invite others to life in Christ.

We are sent in the power of the Holy Spirit; for "those who are called God purifies, and daily gives us strength to bend our thoughts, our skills, our energies, and life itself to this one end" (*The United Methodist Hymnal*, No. 582).

We are sent as congregations of the faithful, to make a corporate witness to God's love and justice in the troubling issues that plague our communities.

We are sent as one household of faith built up in love by the Holy Spirit, inclusive of all who seek the Lord, unified in all our marvelous diversity, having among us one mind, the mind that was in Christ Jesus.

We are sent in the strength and spirit of the United Methodist connection, a covenant that binds all of our congregations in our common mission.

We are sent in the confidence that God will call out new leaders from among our congregations—laity, ordained pastors, missionaries, apostles, prophets, teachers, administrators—to lead and extend our ministries.

We are sent with the vision of God's new creation ever before us.

We are sent in the footsteps of Abraham and Sarah, leaving behind our familiar places and ways of doing things, and risking a journey through the wilderness in faith that God will guide us.

"Go, make of all disciples,"
baptizing in the name
of Father, Son, and Spirit,
from age to age the same.
We call each new disciple
to follow thee, O Lord,
redeeming soul and body
by water and the Word.

Leon M. Adkins
The United Methodist Hymnal, No. 571

Lord, you bless with words assuring:
"I am with you to the end."
Faith and hope and love restoring,
may we serve as you intend
and, amid the cares that claim us,
hold in mind eternity.

With the Spirit's gifts empower us
for the work of ministry.

Jeffery Rowthorn
The United Methodist Hymnal, No. 584

Hope Publishing Co.; 380 S. Main Pl.; Carol Stream, IL 60188.

If a member gets into a problem, be it a death or something else, all church members go to visit him or her or the family. Members take baskets of food or firewood, and they stay with that family some days by taking turns. If a house caught fire, they go to help build another one.

In Burundi, we say that the Parish will look like its leader. If the pastor works hard, the people will work even more.

The United Methodist Church
Nyabugoga-Gitega, Burundi

VITAL CONGREGATIONS—FAITHFUL DISCIPLES

O God,
Open our eyes so that we might see those in our midst who are in need.
Open our ears so that we might hear the cry of the ones who are in anguish.
Open our hearts to the young and old, the rich and poor, the able-bodied and the infirm who are a part of our community.
Help us not only talk about love, but be the ones who are living witnesses to your love as we reach out in love in Christ's name.
Amen.

Trinity Church
Lakewood, California

For the darkness shall turn to dawning,
and the dawning to noon-day bright;
and Christ's great kingdom shall come on earth,
the kingdom of love and light.

H. Ernest Nichol
The United Methodist Hymnal, No. 569

We are sent in the knowledge that, in fellowship with Christ, we are strangers and sojourners on this earth. We are journeying toward a city not made with human hands, eternal in the heavens, the handiwork of God.

There, in communion with all the saints of every time and place, we will praise God forever. "There is a river whose streams make glad the city of God" (Psalm 46:4), and by that river we will live eternally in the radiant presence of God.

From every congregation that gathers in the name of Jesus Christ, a trickle of that river of life flows even now. By its waters, disciples grow up in all ways into Christ. Together these rivulets make a mighty stream of witness to God's salvation.

By water and the Spirit the church is formed and disciples are gathered into communities of witness and service. By water and the Spirit we are now sent to carry on the ministry of Jesus Christ.

May we be blessed by the grace of the Lord Jesus Christ to turn us around and make us whole

And by the love of God to sustain us in every circumstance

And by the communion of the Holy Spirit to lead us and make us one.

APPENDIX A: GLOSSARY

A brief explanation of terms as they are used in this book

Apostolate

The vocation of those sent out by Jesus Christ as messengers of the good news of salvation. Jesus came preaching the gospel of the coming of God's kingdom. He then sent out his followers to do as he was doing, healing the sick and casting out demons (Matthew 10, Mark 6:7-13). After the resurrection, Christ sent the apostles out to preach, teach, and make disciples of all the nations (Matthew 28:18-20). Thus Paul in his calling to take the gospel to the Gentiles referred to himself as an apostle (Romans 1:1). This universal apostolic work belongs to the whole people of God and to every Christian. In all aspects of life and work, Christians are called to witness by word and deed to God's saving love and enduring justice.

See page 56.

Congregation

The gathering or assembly of the people of God for worship, education, and mutual care, for the sake of the mission of Jesus Christ in the world. "Congregation" is close to the literal meaning of the New Testament word *ecclesia*, often translated "church." The *ecclesia* was the assembly of Christians called together by the Lord. Congregations are gatherings of people who have heard the call of Christ to new life and who desire to prepare for carrying on Christ's ministry of healing and reconciliation. Congregations are also social communities of people who stay together across the generations and build up an institutional life of their own. Thus congregations bear a treasure in an earthen vessel (2 Corinthians 4:7) that must be continually cleansed and renewed by the purifying presence of Christ.

See pages 57, 62-64, 66, 73, 74-85.

Connection

The network of covenant relationships that organize and support United Methodist ministry and mission in the world. John Wesley called the meetings of Methodist people and the preachers who led them "the connexion." Their unity was originally expressed in their common personal relationship with Wesley, but later in their meeting together as annual conferences to review Methodist work and teachings. The connection is a spiritual community united in prayer and discipline. The connection is also a network of mutual support for the mission of the church. That mission is expressed through every congregation, every agency or institution of the church, and every individual or corporate effort to extend Christ's ministry in the world. The connection is maintained through general and jurisdictional conferences, and especially by the continual renewing of the covenant in annual conferences. Here ministers are appointed to lead congregations, and agree to serve where sent. Here the congregations commit themselves to supporting the work they have in common, whether locally, regionally, or globally. See *The Book of Discipline, 1988,* ¶112.

See pages 74, 84, 128-29, 139.

Covenant

A bond of trust, commitment, and faithfulness between two or more parties. God initiated the covenant with Abraham and Sarah, and confirmed it through the Exodus. God chose a people to save from exile, so they would live together in mercy and justice as a light to all the nations. Jesus Christ announced a new covenant for all people who would hear the message of salvation and seek to live a new life in Christ. Once no people at all, they became a people of God. Once outside the mercy, now they too received mercy (1 Peter 2:10). John Wesley understood the covenant as both deeply personal and communal. Through Wesley's services of covenant renewal, United Methodists put

VITAL CONGREGATIONS—FAITHFUL DISCIPLES

themselves individually at God's disposal, to do what God calls them to do at whatever sacrifice. They also bind themselves to one another in mutual support, to help one another remain faithful to Christ. Covenants with Christ and with one another are renewed and sealed in the baptism of persons into the family of God, at the table where Christ offers the blood of the new covenant, and in acts of covenant making on Watchnight, in annual conferences, and elsewhere.
See pages 88, 95, 134, 139.

Discernment

A gift of the Spirit enabling one to sift out a finer perception and to see more clearly the direction of God's leading. Discernment requires attention, study, prayer, and openness to the Spirit's guidance. Through discernment one can distinguish an evil or misguided spirit from the Spirit of God (Hebrews 5:14). One can cut through the many possibilities to the truth of how one should act (1 Corinthians 2:14-15). One can learn to read the signs of the times and be strengthened in faithfulness to God's purposes in the world (Luke 12:56). One can see Christ in the broken bread of Holy Communion (1 Corinthians 11:29). And thereby one can also see Christ as well in the brokenness of human life for which the church, Christ's body in the world, now gives its life in service.
See pages 11, 21, 118, 139.

Discipleship

The act of following the teacher of life. Jesus called people to follow, and in following they learned the things that are of greatest truth and value in human life. To be a disciple is to hear the call and to seek to follow Christ by doing as Jesus did. Therefore disciples teach and act on love of God and neighbor, visit the sick and pray for their healing, name and call out the demons that keep people from wholeness of life, sit with prisoners and work for their reconciliation, give help to the poor so they will have good news of hope. To be a faithful disciple is to stay close to the Master. Therefore Christian disciples must discipline their lives in ways that will keep them close to Christ and Christ's ministry.
See pages 54-57, 123-31.

Discipline

A pattern of action that teaches a way of life. The Scriptures describe various patterns that, if practiced over time, begin to shape one's life. Constant prayer, regular fasting, giving to the poor, and continual worship of God are among them. John Wesley learned from spiritual writers of the fourth century that discipline leads to clearer discernment of what God would have one do. As one develops habits of behavior, one grows into dispositions or typical ways of approaching a need or problem. Wesley summed up these dispositions as "perfection in love," in which one approaches every person or situation in a profound attitude of loving as God loves.
See pages 123-31.

Evangelism

Witnessing to the good news of salvation in Christ. Jesus came preaching the gospel (in Greek, *evangelion*) of the kingdom of God. Jesus called people to repentance and conversion, a complete turning around of their lives to face the horizon of God's rule over all creation. Through death on the cross Christ reconciled a sinful humanity with God. Through the resurrection Christ showed the eternity of God's promise of a new creation. Evangelism is the work of the whole people of God. Every Christian is called to witness in word and action to the grace, forgiveness, and love of God. Every Christian is called to live in the light of God's reign, of which Christ's ministry is the sign. Therefore Christians give bread to the hungry, comfort the afflicted, serve the poor, and share their faith with others, that Christ may be known in the world.
See pages 54-55, 122-23, 130-31.

Gift

An ability or capacity a person has received by the grace of God. In the New Testament, the word for *grace* and the word for *gift* is the same *(charism)*. Both mean a

favor, something received, from God. The Holy Spirit bestows the gifts the Christian community needs in order to witness to the gospel (Acts 2). The Spirit provides the special abilities the church needs for mission in the world (1 Corinthians 12:27-30). The Spirit is active in the sacrament of baptism, cleansing and preparing the baptized for ministry. But the faithful disciple must also claim his or her gifts, and as a good steward of what God offers, put them to use in the service of others (1 Peter 4:10). By God's grace, all the gifts of the Christian community when fitted together in the service of the Lord make a unity in building up the body of Christ in love (Ephesians 4:11-16).
See pages 59-60, 90-91, 93-94.

Holiness

The believer's perfecting in love by the grace of God. In the New Testament the saints or "holy ones" were all those in the Christian community who had received new life in Christ. The fruit of that new life is, in John Wesley's term, "holy living." By avoiding evil and seeking to do good, the Christian exhibits the new life that can only come when Christ rules in one's heart. Holiness is also called sanctification or perfection in love. It is an all-embracing way of life. It is both personal as it governs one's thoughts and decisions, and social as it governs relationships in human community. Holiness is a living out of Jesus' great commandments: love of God and love of neighbor.
See pages 70-72.

Kairos

A Greek word meaning the fullness of time. New Testament Greek has two words for time. *Chronos* is time measured by the ticking of a clock or the march of history. For example, a chronology of a congregation is simply the story of its ministry and people over the years. *Kairos* is the fulfillment of time, a moment in time that is rich with meaning. In a *kairos* moment, *chronos* seems to stop. Dreams are fulfilled. Promises are kept. It is as if everything a congregation has done before has been waiting all along just for this moment. A time of *kairos* is a critical moment, a time of decision, an opportunity to move in a new direction. Jesus announced a *kairos*: "The time is fulfilled, and the kingdom of God has come near" (Mark 1:15). Jesus' coming was a *kairos* moment in history. The church's actions in carrying on Jesus' ministry can also be times of *kairos* as they reveal the promise of God's reign.
See pages 17-22.

Laos

A Greek word meaning the people called by God for worship and service in the world. The *laos*, translated into English as laity, is the whole people of God. Unlike an *ethnos*, a racial or "ethnic" group identified by certain physical or cultural features, the *laos* of God may be of any race or culture. Unlike the *hoi polloi*, the undifferentiated crowd of a city street, the *laos* have a distinct identity. The *laos* is a people set apart by a definite calling to witness to the saving love of God (1 Peter 2:10). "Laity" is not a name for people who are not ordained. "Laity" is a name for people called into ministry by virtue of their baptism. God graces the *laos* with gifts for service in the name of the Lord. The laity bear the challenge of carrying Christ's ministry into the everyday life world of work, school, home, and community. Congregations bear a primary responsibility for preparing, training, and supporting the laity for meeting that challenge.
See pages 37-39, 90.

Ministry

Service in the name and after the pattern of Jesus Christ. The New Testament word for ministry is *diakonia*, which comes into English in the word "deacon." In Scripture *diakonia* means simply the service or work done by God's people in helping the poor, feeding the hungry, caring for the sick, or witnessing to Jesus Christ in myriad other ways. Ministry belongs to the whole people of God. Every Christian is called to ministry in baptism, and must discover his or her gifts for ministry bestowed by the Holy Spirit. The Christian community sets apart some

persons for the ordained ministry of preaching the Word, celebrating the sacraments, and administering the work of the church. Others are set apart for special service as diaconal ministers. These roles do not take the place of the ministry of the laity, but rather exist to build up the ministry of God's people in every walk of life.
See pages 84-85, 90-91.

Mission

The tasks for which Christ sends the people of God out across the world. In preaching the kingdom of God, and in dying and rising again as the sign of a new era of history, Jesus Christ created a universal fellowship of faith. Christ sent the apostles out "to all nations" and promised to be with them even to the end of the age Christ had begun (Matthew 28:18-20). The church carries on Christ's mission in every place where people hear the gospel and are touched by the love of God. In every act of feeding the hungry, healing the sick, teaching skills for living, or working for social justice, disciples proclaim the name and saving grace of Jesus Christ. The people of God carry on this work in every land. Thus Christ's mission embraces the globe and makes one universal, ecumenical fellowship of all who seek to follow the Lord.
See pages 62-64, 72, 120-23, 128-29, 142-48.

New Creation

God's transformation of the whole creation into a new order of relationships. In the witness of Scripture, God's new creation is the ultimate promise of a healed and whole reality. In the new creation all divisions are united in the full, loving presence of God. No longer are there male and female, Jew and Gentile, spirit and flesh, sacred and profane, or even night and day (Galatians 3:27-29; Revelation 21:1-4, 22:1-5). All creation comes to fulfillment in the wholeness of God. Christ's rising again from the dead is the first fruit of this new reality. Thus a new era has already begun, to which the church is witness. As the apostle Paul wrote, in Christ there is a new creation (2 Corinthians 5:17). Every believer is baptized into this new creation. Every congregation of the faithful strives to live by God's grace in a form of community that unites what has been divided. Every act of reconciliation is a sign of this new creation that in God's own time will come to fulfillment.
See pages 22, 90, 144-45.

Oikos

A Greek word meaning the household. The New Testament provides a rich vocabulary of connected words with the root word *oikos*. At the most basic level, *oikos* is the family household, not only the physical structure of a house but also those who inhabit it. Scripture refers more broadly to the household of Israel as the whole chosen family of God. Christians build up *(oiko-dome)* a new household filled with the Spirit *(oikos pneumatikos,* 1 Peter 2:5). The church extends God's promise of salvation to the whole inhabited household of earth *(oikoumene)* as one ecumenical family of faith. Ecology *(oikos-logos)* is the proper, harmonious ordering of relationships in the household of earth. The management of the household is called *oikonomia,* the rule *(nomos)* of the house *(oikos).* While *oikonomia* is often translated as stewardship, it is also the root for the word economy. God rules the entire household of earth, and God's plan for transforming that household in Christ is called God's economy (Ephesians 1:9-10). From the family household, to the household of faith, to the ecumenical household, God calls the human family to live by the principles of God's economy.
See pages 60-61.

Reign of God

God's rule governing the earth in mercy, wholeness, justice, and peace. Jesus came announcing that the reign or kingdom of God had come near. Jesus' whole ministry was a revelation of what God's reign is like. The sick are healed, the blind see, the lame walk, the oppressed are liberated, the poor hear good news. When God rules, the sin and brokenness of human life are healed and forgiven. When God rules, people live together in just relationships that create the possibility

of peace. The church is the community of those who seek to follow Christ by giving signs of the Kingdom. By God's grace the Kingdom is present now in acts of healing and reconciliation. In the fullness of time God's reign will be complete and Christ will rule in every heart.
See pages 21, 48, 54-56.

Shalom

A Hebrew word meaning peace, harmony, and well-being in all human relationships. *Shalom* is God's intention for creation. God created human beings to live together in harmony. But there is no peace without just relationships that begin in the family household and extend to all peoples and nations. *Shalom* is defeated by human obsession with security and the raw exercise of power. *Shalom* is created in caring for others, in reconciling hatred, in restraining greed, and in acting for the common good. In all this Jesus Christ is both model and sign. For Christ has broken down the dividing wall of hostility and created one new humanity (Ephesians 2:14-19).

See pages 120-22, 130. See also the 1986 Foundation Document *of the Council of Bishops,* In Defense of Creation, *pages 23-30.*

Sign

A gesture, word, action, or event that points to a greater reality. Jesus brought sight to the blind and words of hope to the poor and outcast. Jesus gave these signs to reveal a much greater reality Jesus had come to announce. Christ's actions were signs pointing to the reign of God in which all sickness would be healed and all injustice would be reconciled. Similarly Christ broke bread and passed the cup at the Last Supper as signs of God's forgiving and reconciling love. Christ's Table is a sign pointing to the heavenly banquet at which all are welcome (Luke 14:16-24). The community of disciples that follows in Christ's footsteps also points to a greater reality. In every word and deed Christians reveal who they believe God is and what they believe Christ's mission is. Through the vitality of congregations and the faithfulness of disciples, God gives the world a sign that Christ is risen and will come again to rule in God's new creation.
See pages 88, 111-39.

Vision

A shared, compelling picture of the future. The Bible offers many pictures of what life is like when God rules the human community. The prophets described a time when the wolf and the lamb would feed together (Isaiah 11:6). Justice would roll down like a waterfall (Amos 5:24). Old and young would dream and see visions of God's reign (Joel 3:1). In his parables Jesus gave glimpses of God's rule in human life. It would be like strangers being welcome at the table of the household, like a parent greeting a long-lost child, like a shepherd going in search of one lost lamb. The vision of the people of God is deeply shaped by these biblical pictures. As congregations plan for the future, they envision ways to make these pictures real. Congregational visions must be concrete. Each congregation must identify and respond to particular needs in the place it has been given to serve. The people must discover and use the unique gifts the Spirit has given them for ministry. Thus vision is an act of discernment. Through study, prayer, and training, the people of God discover how God is leading them to be a sign of the reign of God.
See pages 11, 22, 76, 139.

Vocation

The calling or purpose in life to which one is directed by the Holy Spirit. All Christians receive a vocation in their baptism as they become part of the people of God. This common calling is the "one and the same hope" that all have in Jesus Christ (Ephesians 4:4). All are called to a stewardship of life that directs every action toward the promise of God's new creation. At the same time, the vocation of all God's people takes a particular form for every disciple. The Spirit bestows gifts upon each individual to be used in the service of the Christian community and its mission (1 Peter 4:10). Congregations must help people identify their gifts and discover how to use them as instruments of God's grace.
See pages 59-60, 89-90, 119-20.

APPENDIX B: CONSULTANTS

THE COMMITTEE ON EPISCOPAL INITIATIVES FOR MINISTRY AND MISSION
THE COUNCIL OF BISHOPS

C. P. Minnick, Jr., Chair
Judith Craig
Elias G. Galvan
William Boyd Grove
Leroy C. Hodapp
Felton E. May
Emerito P. Nacpil
Richard B. Wilke

Roy C. Clark, Executive Director

Thomas E. Frank
Principal Writer and Consultant

Helen E. Casey-Rutland
Research Associate

Rollins Center for Church Ministries
Candler School of Theology
Emory University
Atlanta, Georgia, USA

CONSULTANTS

September 1987
Nashville, Tennessee, USA

Maxie Dunnam
Christ United Methodist Church
Memphis, Tennessee

Hae-Jong Kim
District Superintendent
Northern New Jersey Annual Conference

Elizabeth Lopez Spence
Christ United Methodist Church
Albuquerque, New Mexico

Joel Martinez
Emanu-El United Methodist Church
San Antonio, Texas

Tex Sample
St. Paul School of Theology
Kansas City, Missouri

Carol Seckel
District Superintendent
Oregon-Idaho Annual Conference

Roy C. Nichols
Bishop
Special Assignment
Oakland, California

CONSULTANTS

February/March 1989
Atlanta, Georgia, USA

Bruce Birch
Wesley Theological Seminary
Washington, D.C.

David Brownlee
Trinity United Methodist Church
Durham, North Carolina

Anne Broyles
United Methodist Church
Malibu, California

Kirbyjon Caldwell
Windsor Village United Methodist
　Church
Houston, Texas

Sharon A. Brown Christopher
Bishop
Minnesota Area

R. Sheldon Duecker
Bishop
Chicago Area

Charles R. Foster
Candler School of Theology
Atlanta, Georgia

Douglas J. Hall
McGill University
Montreal, Quebec, Canada

George Hunter
Asbury Theological Seminary
Wilmore, Kentucky

Theodore W. Jennings
Bakersfield, California

John Ed Mathison
Frazier Memorial United
　Methodist Church
Montgomery, Alabama

William B. McClain
Wesley Theological Seminary
Washington, D.C.

VITAL CONGREGATIONS—FAITHFUL DISCIPLES

Jorge Pantelis
Calvary United Methodist
  Church
Washington, D.C.

Robert E. Reber
Auburn Theological Seminary
New York, New York

Sharon Ringe
Methodist Theological School
in Ohio
Delaware, Ohio

John Ripley
First United Methodist Church
Oak Ridge, Tennessee

Louis W. Schowengerdt
Bishop
New Mexico Area

Rodney T. Smothers
Central United Methodist Church
Atlanta, Georgia

Howard A. Snyder
United Theological Seminary
Dayton, Ohio

Leonard I. Sweet
United Theological Seminary
Dayton, Ohio

David L. Watson
General Board of Discipleship
Nashville, Tennessee

Other Consultants

Paul Dietterich
Inagrace Dietterich
Center for Parish Development
Chicago, Illinois

Carl Dudley
McCormick Seminary
Chicago, Illinois

STAFF CONSULTANTS

James Craig
Eli Rivera
Board of Global Ministries

Jack A. Keller, Jr.
United Methodist Publishing
  House

Ezra Earl Jones
Duane A. Ewers
General Board of Discipleship

William R. Richards
Roger Burgess
Don Hughes
United Methodist Communications

C. David Lundquist
General Council on Ministries

CONSULTANTS

AREA ADVISORY COMMITTEES

Over eight hundred laity and clergy have been involved in discussion of the Episcopal Initiative and in reading the first draft of the *Foundation Document*. Each Bishop asked a layperson and pastor from each of up to ten congregations to serve on an Area Advisory Committee.

Congregations were selected by each Bishop to represent the broad range of local churches in her or his episcopal area. Nearly three hundred of those congregations conducted "A Gathering for Celebration and Discovery" and returned a response form to the Council of Bishops. The wonderful array of stories, images, and prayers that came back on these forms is represented throughout this book.

A PASTORAL LETTER TO ALL UNITED METHODISTS

From your sisters and brothers in Christ Jesus, The Council of Bishops, to the people called United Methodist around the world: grace to you and peace in the name of our Lord Jesus Christ.

We the bishops of the church declare our commitment to congregational vitality and faithful discipleship. We invite you to join us as we claim the gifts of the Spirit offered to us by the Lord Jesus, who is the foundation of our ministry and the source of all vitality and all faithfulness.

While our church is global and connectional, we believe that the central expression of ministry and mission in Christ's name is the local congregation. Here the gospel is preached and taught; here the sacraments are celebrated; here the offerings of the people are given and received; here discipleship finds its source and its direction. To our congregations we address this pastoral letter and the Foundation Document which accompanies it, *Vital Congregations—Faithful Disciples*.

United Methodist people are scattered across the planet earth, living under highly diverse political, economic and cultural systems. All of us gather in local congregations. From Germany to the Philippines, from Scandinavia to Mozambique, from the eastern seaboard of the United States over the hillsides of Appalachia across the prairies of the American Midwest to the coastlands of the West, our people hear the historic yet contemporary call to "reform the continent(s) and to spread scriptural holiness over the land(s)."

We, the people of God called United Methodist, have come to a critical turning point in our history. The world in which our heritage of faith seemed secure is passing away. We must choose to be faithful to Jesus Christ in our time.

There are many signs within our congregations that we recognize this new era. The realization is dawning on us that we must be more intentional about being the church God calls us to be. The immense suffering of so many people in the world today overwhelms us, but these human hurts also stir our deepest impulse to follow our master into service and fellowship with those who suffer.

As teachers and pastors who are charged with the spiritual and temporal leadership of the church, we are privileged to share with you our vision for the church in our time. What we offer to the church is not a program or a grand master plan. We envision a blessed connection of vital congregations that seek to respond in unique and individual ways to the command of our Lord to teach, to baptize, and to make disciples. We envision vital congregations that claim Christ's promise to be with us (Matthew 28). Our vision, then, is an invitation to journey toward vitality and faithfulness.

We believe that the signs of vital faith can be revealed each time a congregation gathers to worship God; thus, our Foundation Document is a reflection of the nature of those gatherings. When we worship as congregations, we sing and pray. We confess our sin and receive forgiveness. We hear the Word proclaimed. We are baptized and witness the baptism of others. We are fed at the Table of the Lord. We are sent forth to share the good news of God's amazing grace. These elements of our worship must become the pattern of our everyday life in the world.

We the bishops of the church yearn for a vital congregation in every place. We yearn because so many people of our societies, including many in our church, have no vital relationship to God, and are lost: lost to drug addiction, lost to self-centered materialism and self-righteousness, lost to the demonic forces of racism and every form of human oppression—lost to sin. We are concerned that as our world becomes more secularized, new generations increasingly are bewildered by every form of temptation and desperately need the saving grace of Christ.

Jesus came and comes to seek and to save those who are lost, and the church is called to be the extension of the Incarnation, Christ's life in the midst of the world. Thus, we yearn for a vital congregation in every place.

As bishops we commit ourselves
- to fast and pray on behalf of congregational vitality and faithful discipleship;
- to lead our annual conferences in discerning God's vision for the church and congregational life;
- to evaluate our styles of episcopal leadership as they affect congregational life and the mission of the connection;
- to seek to nurture the life of existing congregations and to encourage the establishment of new ones;
- to preach the Word and celebrate Holy Communion regularly in local congregations.

We plead with you to join us in our yearning, in our fasting, in our praying, in our study and in our work on behalf of vital congregations and faithful disciples, and in commending Jesus Christ as Lord and Savior to the world.

VITAL CONGREGATIONS—FAITHFUL DISCIPLES

We call each pastor and lay leader to engage the congregation in study of our Foundation Document and issues of congregational vitality. We urge local congregations to seek God's vision for the church through earnest listening to the Word of God in Scripture. We call our people to disciplined missional prayer on behalf of our church and its congregations.

Let us, as the people of God, join in this act of seeking new vision for the church, so that we may discern who God would have us be and what God would have us do as faithful disciples of Jesus Christ gathered into vital congregations, and scattered for ministry in the world.

As we the bishops conclude this pastoral letter we offer prayers for all of you and for our congregations worshiping and witnessing in every land.

We pray that God will use this episcopal initiative and the lives and gifts of all of us on behalf of the gospel that the world may believe and be saved. "Now to the One who is able to do immeasurably more than all that we ask or think through the power that is at work among us, to God be glory in the church and in Christ Jesus to all generations forever and ever." Amen (Ephesians 3:20-21).